SPACE BATTLE

Duruy sat at the calculating table, with the intercom headset clamped over his ears. There was the gentlest pressure at the small of his back as Project Excelsior swung slowly through the arc that would bring her torpedo tubes to bear on the enemy.

Etchardy's voice carried a string of figures to his ears: "Azimuth two-zero-point-one-six; line zero-zero-point-seven-one; elevation no change; azimuth two-one-point-zero-two . . ."

The skin felt tight over Duruy's face and his head ached from twelve uninterrupted hours of concentrated labor at the big board. In seconds, it would all be over, one way or the other.

—And then the space station rocked with a violent, volcanic shock.

DOUBLE IN SPACE

TWO NOVELS
BY FLETCHER PRATT

MODERN LITERARY EDITIONS PUBLISHING COMPANY
NEW YORK, N.Y.

Copyright 1951 by Standard Magazines, Inc.

Published by arrangement with Doubleday & Company, Inc.

All of the characters in this book are fictitious, and any resemblance to actual persons, living or dead, is purely coincidental.

"The Wanderer's Return," originally published in December, 1951, *Thrilling Wonder Stories*.

"Project Excelsior," originally published in October, 1951, *Thrilling Wonder Stories* as "Asylum Satellite."

PROJECT EXCELSIOR

I

☐ They sat together on the broad veranda with the light from within gilding the curl of smoke from Duruy's cigarette, watching how white curls of foam sped up out of the dark Atlantic to hurl themselves against the beach below the balustrade. Overhead the stars of the Southern Hemisphere marched in a tremendous parade; but as they watched, one, more brilliant than all the others and perceptibly round, slowly climbed above the eastern rim of sea.

Bennett-Drax lifted his *gintônico*, and in the lazy accent that seemed to comport so oddly with being a secret agent, said, "Here's to your future home, old man."

"Here's to it," said Duruy, and drank. Then: "But 'home' is rather the wrong word, isn't it? I don't expect to stay any longer than just enough to get the new calculator running smoothly."

"You can't always say, you know," said Bennett-Drax. His voice dropped a trifle. "With so many of them being hit by the two-fifties . . ."

His voice trailed off as the opening of the door left them suddenly surrounded by a blare of syncopation from the Copacabana's orchestra, and a man came out, looked along the line of the veranda, and then came hurrying toward them, hand outstretched.

"Senhor Lambert!" he cried. "What a joyous meeting! Judge my delight when I learn that you are not only in

Copyright, 1951, by Standard Magazines, Inc. Originally published in October, 1951, *Thrilling Wonder Stories* as "Asylum Satellite."

Rio, but precisely in this hotel where we celebrate a happy occasion. Do us the honor to be one of our party." Duruy accepted the proffered hand and turned toward Bennett-Drax, who had risen with him. "Peter," he said, "this is Senhor Herculeo Maricá. We were in the calculations branch together at M.I.T., before I went to White Sands. Senhor Maricá, Peter Bennett-Drax, British Empire Motors."

"Enchanted," said the Brazilian. "Will you also do us the honor? A small party, but truly an occasion that will become memorable by your acceptance."

"Well, I don't know——" began the Englishman, but Duruy cut in with, "Oh, come on, Peter. The vacation's about over, anyway, and I need one good party under my belt before getting back to work." He turned to Maricá. "But I thought you were up in Goiás somewhere, building sun-power motors."

"So I was," said Maricá, his teeth flashing in a smile. "I flew in but yesterday. And I thought you, my friend, were up above us there in that incredible artifical moon of yours."

Bennett-Drax cleared his throat. "I came back," said Duruy briefly. "What's the occasion of the celebration, Herculeo?"

"The wedding of the daughter of the interventor of Santa Catarina to a cousin of mine. In this direction."

He steered them across the lobby and up the stairs to the floor which the Copacabana reserves for the private parties of the very rich or very important. A small orchestra was playing at the end of the room they entered, and a girl in a flouncy but highly revealing costume was revolving gracefully to the paces of the *onça*, her castanets clicking. At the opposite end a table was piled with food and busy waiters were opening champagne. In between, about a hundred people in evening dress were talking animatedly, not paying the slightest attention to the dancer.

Marciá guided Duruy and Bennett-Drax through the press and introduced them to the bridegroom, who wore the uniform of the Brazilian Rocket Service, and the bride, who had the beginnings of a mustache, then two or three others, before taking them to the champagne table. There was a patter of applause as the dancer finished; Duruy heard Bennett-Drax beside him say in a low tone, "It looks all right, but you can't tell who you'll run into in a crowd as big as this." He felt a momentary surge of irritation, and was just turning round to tell the agent to lay off being a sleuth for a moment when it happened.

She was standing at the other side of the room, head tilted slightly and one hand lifted as she listened to something the man in front of her was saying. Duruy never saw the man at all; it did not seem worth while looking at anything but the lovely head, so proudly held, with its helmet of coal-black hair and the white shoulders that went down into a gown of deep blue which looked as though it had been cast upon her. There was a jewel in her hair. Duruy gave a slight gasp and gulped champagne.

Maricá beside him said, "What disturbs you, my friend? You look as though you had seen a miracle."

Duruy managed a grin. "I think perhaps I have seen the girl I am in love with. Who is she?"

Maricá followed his glance. "And imagine that they say the Anglo-Saxons are unemotional! She is a Castelhoso, I think. They have an enormous fazenda in the mountain country, up in Paraná. Would you like to meet her?"

"I knew there must be some reason why I came here. Yes."

"Wait."

As the Brazilian threaded his way toward the group that contained the girl, Bennett-Drax said, "Look here, old man——"

Duruy made a gesture of impatience. "Yes, I know, I'm so valuable it hurts because I know so much about the space station, and you're keeping me from harm. But life has to go on just the same, and this is an emotional matter. You can look her up."

Maricá was beckoning from across the room. Duruy put down his glass and moved toward where he was waiting, the girl on one side, the man she had been talking with on the other. "Senhorita Castelhoso, may I present Senhor Duruy? Senhor Mascarenas, Senhor Duruy. He was a member of the first party on what they call Project Excelsior, the new star in our heavens."

Her hand lay cool and soft in his. "Only one of the new stars," he said. "After all, the Russians have one, too, and"—he hesitated a second and then, yes, Brazilians always expected to be complimented—"there are also stars here on earth."

She laughed beautifully. "You have been in our country long enough to learn that its women demand flattery. But I warn you I see through it. I was educated in Paris."

The orchestra had swung into a slow waltz and couples were sliding out on the floor. "Shall we dance?" he said; she nodded and put up her arms.

They danced and talked about Paris. They drank champagne and talked about people they might know. They danced again and talked about everything he could think of. He found she was interested in books, art, music, and had a highly developed critical taste in all three, with a certain gift of quaintly humorous expression. Then she was tired of dancing, and he suggested they sit on the terrace.

"Where did you learn so much about the arts?" he asked, when they were seated.

"Oh, in Paraná, in the mountains, there is so little else to do. We take the journals. It is like you in your space station." She pointed up to where, overhead now, Project Excelsior loomed like a diminutive moon in its three-quarter phase. "Did you not find time for much reading while you were there?"

For the first time he hesitated. "Well, I——"

"Oh, I know. The space station of the Western Allies is all most terribly secret, and you are not allowed to talk about it, and you even have that bodyguard following you like a big English mastiff. He is probably peering around a corner at us this moment, asking himself whether I seduce you or the reverse. But I ask no pardons. It is only that I wished to hear about your life there in the sky, and how it is lonely, like mine in the hills."

"Oh." Duruy put his relief into his voice. "Well, I suppose the most important thing about a space station is that you're so busy all the time with what's happening to your body that you can't do anything with your mind. At least that was the way I felt. You may get used to it later; I was only there a short time."

"Is it strange, then, the sensation?"

"Very strange. The weightlessness makes some people sick. In fact it makes everyone sick at first, and the supply rocket always has to stay around for three or four days to take back anyone that doesn't get over it. And there isn't any time except artificially. You do a lot of sleeping. The psychs have found out that maximum human efficiency under the conditions is on a routine of eight hours sleeping and twelve hours on duty, so things are arranged that way—in a twenty-hour day. It may be different on the Russian station. Theirs is black on the outside, you know."

"And no cultural life?"

"How can there be? A few books, and I remember one of the machinists had a mouth organ while I was there. But there isn't room for any movies or things like that."

"I should think the radio or television——"

"Oh, didn't you know—I'm afraid I can't talk about that, though." Duruy sighed. "There's such a hell of a lot I'd like to tell you about it, and I can't say a word. . . .

Do I get a chance to see you tomorrow?"

She placed one hand on his arm. "If you wish."

"I'll probably have to bring Bennett-Drax with me as a chaperon. What do you say to the concert, and then we can have dinner? I'm on a vacation and free as air."

She smiled. "For Senhor Bennett-Drax I will provide a distraction. There is the daughter of the people I am staying with. The address is Rua de Albuquerque 16. And now, the hour, what is it? I fear they will be looking for me."

Duruy conducted her back into the ballroom, now thinning of guests and acquiring that indescribably raffish atmosphere which attends on rooms where parties have been held. As she had predicted, Bennett-Drax was waiting just inside the door, his face wearing the vacant expression that to Duruy's experienced eye foretold stormy weather.

He was quite right. When they had reached their own room the Englishman said, "I really don't like to put on you, old man, but I would advise against it, I fear."

"I expected as much," said Duruy, taking off his jacket. "You're like a doctor; you advise against anything but a diet of milk, eggs, and oatmeal, regular hours and exercise with the dumbbells."

"I would not refer to association with the young lady as exercise with a dumbbell," said Bennett-Drax. "Her first name is Tina."

"I found that out. After all, it isn't polite to address your friends by their last names in Brazil."

"She's staying with some people named Guycochéa at Rua de Albuquerque 16."

"I found that out too. You and I are going there tomorrow afternoon and take her and the Guycochéa girl to a concert."

"Indeed." Bennett-Drax lifted his eyebrows slightly. "The rapidity of your progress amazes me. What I was going to say was that those two scraps of information constitute practically the entire dossier on the lady as of even date. I called old Rolim at the Polícia Segrêda. He doesn't know any Castelhosos from Paraná."

Duruy stopped undressing and faced around. "Look here, Peter," he said, "because she's lived so quietly off there in the back blocks that they haven't got a file on her, does that mean she's a Russian agent? Don't be silly. I talked with her all evening. She speaks a straight and very good brand of Brazilian Portuguese, and she's spent so much time on things like books and music that there wouldn't be enough left for her to do any agenting."

"That's how they train them these days, my friend. Remember Siyard the chess player, and how he tried to get away with the plans for the Flying Dragon rocket when he was giving that exhibition at Princeton?"

"This is nothing like that. I haven't any plans, and even if I had, I don't see how she could get them away from me. You must have a low opinion of my loyalty."

Bennett-Drax put out a hand. "I have a low opinion of your discretion. Not that you'd talk out of turn, even to a girl. But you know altogether too much about the arrangements at the station and about the range-and-charge calculator for the torpedoes. The Russkis are crazy to find out some of the details. We have our own agents inside some of their organizations and a pretty good lead on what they want, you know that. I'm not trying to protect you, just the contents of your brain. If they get hold of you they'll find some means of extracting them. I can't help finding it suspicious when an acquaintance is formed this easily, that's all."

"All right." Duruy's anger dissolved in a grin. "Chaperon me all you want to. Plant agents of the Segrêda behind the bushes in the park so I don't tell secrets when we're out for a walk. But I've only got a week before I take off for that biscuit up there in the sky, and I want to have a little fun. I might not come back, you know. There are the two-fifties."

II

☐ "I have never tasted anything so good in my life," said Duruy. "It is not like the way you Brazilians usually do meat."

"Oh, we have resources you North Americans do not dream of," said Tina Castelhoso. "But this is not really a Brazilian recipe at all. I learned it in Paris from an old Hungarian woman there. It is called by a name I always find it hard to pronounce—Zigrana, Zingara. But I'd rather eat it than talk it, anyway."

"What's the meat?"

"Veal."

She got up, produced two plates of frozen *creame de abacate* salad, and sat down again, looking at her plate.

Duruy stopped eating and contemplated her for a moment. Then he said, "Tina." He could feel that his own voice was a trifle unsteady.

The fading light struck almost level through the window, and in it he could see the little muscles at the base of her nostril move slightly. "What is it?" she said, without looking up.

"Have I offended you somehow?"

"No—oh no." Suddenly both hands came up to her face and she was crying, twisting out of her chair and to her feet.

Duruy's own chair went over backward as he leaped up and around the little table to take her in his arms. She clung to him desperately, the dark head pillowed on his shoulder, sobbing without words. After a minute or two, as the tempo of her weeping decreased, he lifted her face in his two hands and kissed the tears from her eyes, then began to kiss her on the lips, hard and hard. She reciprocated avidly for a time, pushed him gently away, and said in an ordinary tone:

"Have you a handkerchief? I must look like an Argentine actress."

"You look beautiful. Tina, will you marry me?"

The nostril muscle jumped again, and she put out one hand to him. "Lambert, I wish I could. Come, sit down, we must talk this out."

The rest of the meal she had cooked for him forgotten, she led the way to the couch. Through the window Corcovado with its huge statue of Christ was just catching the last rays of the sun.

"Tina, I love you." He reached out to take her hand, and she let him, but passively.

"Lambert, I am thinking I love you too, but it cannot do. I must go back to Paraná, and you must go away, I do not know where."

"Come with me."

"No. I cannot."

"What is there to prevent, if we love each other?"

She caught her breath. "It is—a family matter. I cannot tell you."

She avoided his effort to take her in his arms again. With a horrible sense of futility, he cried, "Isn't there anything at all that will make you change your mind?"

"No. But——" She looked at the floor and in the gathering dusk he was surprised to see her cheeks suddenly flame red.

"What is it, Tina?"

"It has been so beautiful a week, and now it will end tomorrow. Ah, Lambert, we will have only a memory. . . . I have thought of something. Do you know the Guycochéas have a villa up in the mountain at Petropolis?

It is called the Villa Cedrosa, and is not open now, only in the summer season, in January. A red building, set back from the street, on the Avenida Bembom."

Duruy felt his heart pounding. "Well?" he said.

"I could get the keys from Dolores. Would you—could you—get a car and meet me there tonight?"

This time he swept her into his arms before she could protest, but after a minute she disengaged herself and said gently, "Not now. It is about an hour and a half of driving. I will be there as soon as Dolores comes home and I can get the keys and her car. I——"

There was a step in the hall and the door opened on Senhor Guycochéa. Confound it, thought Duruy as they went through the formal inquiries about each other's health and he prepared to leave, of all times to interrupt! Tina came with him to the door; as she turned away after an almost whispered "Until tonight," he thought he caught the gleam of another teardrop in her eye, and decided that she was the most enigmatic as well as the loveliest girl he had ever known.

It was past sunset when he reached the street, but there was an all-night garage on the Ipanema where, after prolonged haggling over the amount of the deposit, and the proprietor's call to the Copacabana to verify the fact that Duruy really lived there, he was able to acquire an ancient 1957 model Buick. There wasn't time to go back to the hotel, he decided, and if he did, Bennett-Drax would probably put his foot down on the idea of an unaccompanied nocturnal expedition, anyway. And Duruy could hardly explain. Well, let the big lug of a British watchdog worry for one night. He had been trying all week to get something on Tina and hadn't been able to turn up a single thing to her discredit. Several people had seen her at various social functions, and the Guycochéas, with whom she was staying, were well known in Rio; one of them was even a secretary of legation at some Brazilian diplomatic post abroad.

As the car left the city boundary and swung into the steeper and less well paved road up the mountainside to Petropolis, Duruy wondered if Tina were ahead of him, and addressed himself to the curious problem of her behavior. What strange influence was it that led her to accept his love, yet refuse to marry him and declare that this night must be their last? Religion? She had never mentioned it. Some fear that she did not want to be tied up with a man engaged in the rather desperate business of a trip out to Project Excelsior? If she knew he was going, she must have found out elsewhere. The station in space hadn't even been mentioned by either of them since that first night. She said it was a family matter; it could be she was promised in marriage to some old buzzard of a politico, who had a hold on the family. Brazilians were always getting mixed up in deals like that. But then, why couldn't she tell him about it? He made up his mind to ask her again, and more urgently, for some explanation. There was always, or nearly always, some way around things, and he wasn't going to give her up, no matter what her background and problems.

Ahead, as he reached a comparatively level stretch, his lights picked out a big black car, parked so that it occupied a good half of the narrow road. Duruy swore and reduced speed. As he drew abreast of the machine he saw that one of the occupants was in the other half of the road with uplifted hand and slowed to a stop.

It was a small, thin Brazilian, who leaned on the side of the Buick. "*Faç favor*," he said. "Does the senhor have mechanical knowledge?"

"Not enough to fix a breakdown, I'm afraid," said Duruy. "And besides, if you don't mind, I'm in a terrible——"

He heard the click of the opposite door behind him and turned to find himself looking into the muzzle of a steadily held automatic.

"You will descend," said the voice behind it in precisely pronounced English.

Duruy swung his head. The small, thin Brazilian had a gun too. He descended, calling himself seventeen hundred kinds of a jackass. Was Tina . . . ?

"You will proceed along the path to the right," said the voice. A flashlight gleamed past him to show a flagged walk between a double lane of dwarf mimosas. "Do not attempt to run, my friend. There are several of us, and you will merely give us the inconvenience of transporting you by another means. We will not shoot."

Duruy heard other feet behind him. There were several of them. He also heard the clash of gears as somebody started the rented Buick. They were taking no chances.

The flagged path ended at the door of a house which appeared to be low and rambling. One of Duruy's conductors opened it and switched on a light to reveal a hall luxuriously furnished in the Brazilian style. He was prodded across it and into a room at one side, which the light revealed as fitted for a doctor's office.

"Sit down, Mr. Duruy," said one of his captors. There were four of them. The one who had spoken English was big and rather blond, with a broad face; Slav probably, Duruy decided. The other three looked like Brazilians. They were the ones with the weapons.

The big one switched to Portuguese. "We are going to ask you some questions, Senhor Duruy. You will answer in Portuguese for the benefit of these gentlemen, who do not understand your native language."

"Oh yes," said Duruy. "And I suppose that if I don't answer you'll turn on the heat."

The big man said, "Soviet science has developed many methods of insuring that people tell the truth, but we are in a hurry at present." He had stepped to a medicine cabinet and was busily filling a hypodermic with a colorless liquid.

"Scopolamine!" said Duruy.

"An improved derivative. Put out your arm."

"I'll be damned if I do," said Duruy, leaped to his feet, and lunged suddenly at the big man. He might as well have spared himself the trouble. The big man avoided him neatly, one of the other three kicked him in the shins, another jumped on his back, and down he went in a tangle of legs and arms that presently resolved itself into a Duruy spread-eagled on the floor. One of the men quickly and neatly tied his ankles together, another applied a hammer lock to his right arm and guided him to the chair, while the third held his left wrist.

The big man sighed. "It is characteristic of the decadent peoples to expend their strength in futile effort," he said. "Senhor Duruy, we have been following you for weeks. We could have taken you at any time since you arrived in Rio, but it would have involved slightly more inconvenience because of the large Englishman. Now I advise you to behave well. It will make the experience much easier."

He picked up the needle again and advanced. "All right," said Duruy, "but tell me one thing. Did Tina Castelhoso have anything to do with this? I've got to know."

The big man checked, and his face showed something like surprise. "The young lady you have been seeing so frequently? What emotional instability you Americans show! I am not authorized to give you this information.

She hadn't, Duruy thought, as he winced under the prick of the needle. The man who had the hammerlock on him whipped a cord round the wrist and tied the arm to the chair, the other followed suit with the left arm, and all three stood back to admire their work. One of them got another chair and produced a notebook and a fountain pen.

The drug was quick-acting. Duruy felt a kind of grayness settle over his mind, as though he were dreaming and conscious of dreaming, but somehow couldn't manage to wake up. The big man sat down and addressed him:

"Your name is Lambert Duruy, is it not?"

"Yes."

"You were in the first crew on the space station called Project Excelsior?"

"Yes."

"What is the armament of the station?"

"It mounts twenty-four rocket-powered winged torpedoes."

"Do they have atomic war heads?"

"Yes."

"Can they be directed to any spot on earth?"

"Yes."

"Can the station vary its orbit around the earth?"

"Yes."

"What is the means of communicating with the station?"

"Radar."

"What was your position aboard?"

"Calculator operator for the torpedoes."

"Do you expect to go back?"

"Yes."

"When?"

"In three weeks."

"Is not the present calculator operator satisfactory?"

"Yes."

"Why are they replacing him with you?"

"To keep him from getting the two-fifties."

"What is that?"

"Radiation disease from cosmic rays."

"You have no means of preventing that?"

"No."

"Nor of curing it?"

"No."

Through the gray haze of the drug Duruy saw satisfaction painted on the faces of the four men watching him. The big man leaned closer and looked at him intently.

"What means does Project Excelsior use to prevent the attack of meteorites?"

"None."

This seemed to throw them. They glanced from one to another in bewilderment. One of the men said, "Is the injection wearing off?"

"Not in this time," said the big man. "I don't understand it. He must have taken a counterinjection."

"Ask him."

"No. If he is lying one time, he could lie again. No. The treatment simply is not working well. We will have to get him away from here to some place where we can apply other methods."

One of the three ran a tongue around his lips. "I do not like this," he said. "The Segrêda——"

"It is——"

There was a shot outside.

The big man jumped up, upsetting his chair. One of the other three leaped for the door, the other two bounded to Duruy's side. A whistle blew shrilly.

"Hold them back," cried the big man, and in three strides disappeared through the door at the back of the room. Duruy heard a heavy pounding, then the crash as the outer door was broken through and another shot. The doctor's office door was burst in and a swarm of armed men in the green uniform of the Segrêda poured through it to cover the pair that had been standing guard over Duruy.

"Are you hurt, senhor?" one of them asked.

"No," said Duruy dully, and one of the other Segrêda agents came close, looked at his eyes for a moment, and said; "He has been drugged. Inform Senhor Bennett-Drax."

III

☐ Lambert Duruy sat in the office at White Sands and, although it was most thoroughly air-conditioned, was aware of perspiration trickling along the lines of his palms. On one side of the big desk facing him was a small silk American flag in a metal holder; on the other was a model of the space rocket *Goddard*, used for the periodic trips to Project Excelsior; and between them was a little plate which proclaimed that the desk belonged to "Gen. Chr. Gebhard." It reminded Duruy of a butcher's sign he had seen when he was a boy in New Orleans, only that belonged to "Chr. Behrman."

Gen. Chr. Gebhard was not behind the desk. Duruy turned his head to where Bennett-Drax sat, a picture of British aloofness and calm, but there didn't seem anything to say, so he said nothing.

The door opened and a little group came in, headed by General Gebhard, a short, square man with a white brush-cut above a pink face. The two earlier arrivals scrambled to their feet and there were introductions—Brigadier General Keyes of Rocket Ordnance, Colonel le Maistre, G-2 of the Western Alliance, Major General Fuller, Operations, and a Lieutenant Tinkham, who proceeded to set up a recorder.

A little silence as all took their places, and Gebhard said, "I think that for the record you should describe the sequence of events, Captain."

"Very well," said Bennett-Drax. He spoke in an even,

unemotional voice. "Mr. Duruy was dining out and I was expecting his return to the hotel—the Copacabana—when I received a telephone call. It was a woman's voice."

Colonel le Maistre raised a hand. "Did you recognize the voice, Captain?"

"No," said Bennett-Drax, "but I'm afraid that is not significant. She spoke in French. There's no one even remotely connected with the case who speaks French normally, and it's very easy to disguise a voice by using another language. She seemed in a great hurry. As nearly as I can recall, she said, 'Duruy is going to Petropolis tonight to meet someone. Stop him quickly. Tell him he is on no account to go, he will never arrive.' "

Le Maistre said, "Did you have the call traced?"

"I called the hotel switchboard—the Segrêda has a girl there—and said I wanted it traced, but that led to nothing. It was made from a pay station in the casino of the Paulista and there are so many people drifting in and out there that no one could remember."

"Go on."

"It occurred to me to wonder why Duruy would never arrive. Obviously, because someone knew he was going and he would be waylaid en route. I called the place where Duruy was dining——"

"Where was it?" said General Gebhard. "This is for the record."

Duruy himself answered, "At the apartment of some people named Guycochéa in Rua de Albuquerque, with a Miss Castelhoso."

Bennett-Drax took up the narration. "There was no answer, so I assumed he had already left. It seemed to me that pursuit would provide only a rather poor sequence for the video, since I would arrive only in time to discover the body if the purpose of our friends were assassination, and if it were not, they would have to remove him to some building to extract the information they wanted. I went round to Colonel Rolim of the Segrêda and asked him whether he had on his lists any suspicious buildings out the road to Petropolis. He said he certainly did; that the Villa Aldobrandini directly on the road was occupied by a doctor who never had any patients, and who was assuredly a letter drop for the Russian espionage network. The Segrêda had let him alone—keeping him in the wings, as it were, until they wanted him for a star turn. As this seemed a good one, Rolim and I buzzed out there with a couple of carloads of Segrêda agents. We found Duruy, trussed up like a fowl and answering questions under drugs; also a couple of Russian agents, live; also another pair who weren't worth bringing back, because they were in a poor state of repair when we got through with them."

"And the doctor?" Colonel le Maistre asked.

"Slipped away from us. The Segrêda isn't very gentle, and extracted from the other two the information that his real name is Gavril Mahovitzov, as well as a list of his usual hiding places. They'll doubtless lay him by the heels in a day or so."

There was another momentary silence. General Gebhard said, "Mr. Duruy, you must surely realize that this puts you in a very equivocal position. What was your reason for leaving the captain, assigned to protect you, and going off in the direction of Petropolis?"

Duruy felt his face flush and his hands were wet with perspiration. General Keyes was regarding him grimly. He said, "In the service we would call it desertion in the face of the enemy."

"I——" began Duruy, and then stopped. "Do you doubt my loyalty, sir?" he cried wildly.

"No," said the general, "but——"

Colonel le Maistre pulled a long French mustache, and there was a twinkle in his eye as he addressed Gebhard: "*Mon Général*, I suggest that this line of inquiry is unfruitful. In my country it would be at once recognized that we are dealing here with an affair of the heart, and a young man who seeks to protect someone's name." He turned to Bennett-Drax. "Does not the evidence you have support this?"

"It does," said the Englishman decisively. "When Mr. Duruy made the acquaintance of this Miss Castelhoso with whom he dined on the evening he was kidnaped, I warned him that the account of her antecedents was vague and unsatisfactory. On the morning after the event Colonel Rolim and I went round to the Guycochéas', where she was staying. They said that she had left to go back to Paraná on the previous evening in a state of great agitation. They have known her only about four months. The Segrêda has the question of tracing her in hand."

General Keyes's mouth set in a line as thin and accurate as though drawn by a ruler. "Court-martial him," he snapped.

"I think not—yet," said Gebhard. "Mr. Duruy has been extremely indiscreet, and may consider himself severely reprimanded. But there is no reason to doubt his loyalty, and you must remember he is one of the few men who can operate the torpedo calculator." He turned to General Fuller. "Is there anyone else you would trust with it?"

"Not with the new machine that guides the Mark VII torpedo. All the others show consistent twenty-five-mile errors. It takes a rather peculiar brain, like that for playing chess."

"Very well," said Gebhard, and turned to Duruy again. "How much did you tell this woman?"

Duruy writhed under the contempt in the last word, and felt as though he were being stipped naked and put under a glass. "Nothing," he said. "She knew I had been out to Project Excelsior—Herculeo Maricá told her that when he introduced us. But she didn't even know I was going back, and we never talked about it."

"Ah!" Colonel le Maistre pulled at his mustache again and took up the inquiry. "Then we address ourselves to the questioning given you at the Villa Aldobrandini, which is evidently the key of the situation. Let us discover how much has been learned, and consider what we may deduce from this thirst for information. How much of it do you remember?"

"A good deal," said Duruy. "As soon as I came out of it, Peter—Captain Bennett-Drax had me set down everything I remembered, and I've been rattling my brains since, trying to fill in the gaps."

"Good. And what was the line of questioning?"

"Well, first they wanted to know the armament of the station, whether the torpedoes had atomic heads, and whether they could be directed to any spot on earth."

"Doubtless test questions merely," said Le Maistre. "They cannot be ignorant of these things. And then?"

"Whether the station could vary its orbit."

"Ah! We approach. Gentlemen, I submit that this indicates the Russian station cannot vary its orbit."

"Too long a jump," said Keyes, but Fuller said, "There hasn't been any perturbation or variation in the orbit of the Russian station since they sent it up, and it's outside ours, which means that if they could get it in to give their torpedoes a shorter and better run, they'd do it. I consider the colonel's deduction justified. What came next, Duruy?"

"They asked me a lot about the two-fifties, sir. Whether we had any means of preventing or curing it. I was pretty groggy, but I thought they seemed very much pleased when I said we didn't."

"Therefore, the Russians do have such a means, or are on the track of it," said Le Maistre. "What then?"

"They asked me what we did to keep meteorites from hitting the station."

"Did you tell them?"

"I couldn't help it."

"But certainly. You are not held in fault for this. And the next?"

"About that time Captain Bennett-Drax and the Segrêda came in and they had something else to think about. They were still arguing over the fact I said we did nothing about meteorites when he arrived. Didn't believe it. The doctor, the one who gave me the shot in the arm, said I must have taken a counterinjection to prevent my reacting to their dope."

Le Maistre leaned back in his chair and tugged at his mustache thoughtfully. "And he is the one who escapes," he murmured.

"I'm glad they didn't get anything more out of you," said Keyes, with a closer approach to cordiality than anything he had shown.

"Do not interrupt," said the Frenchman. "I am following the rabbit into its den and the pieces begin to fit together. . . . Regard, now: the Russian does not credit the statement that our station is without protection against meteorites. Yet theirs cannot vary its orbit. It is much farther out than ours, and we know from observation that it is surrounded by huge plates of dark metal. Does it not follow that they have placed their station where it stands to reduce the arrival velocity of meteorites? And consequently, that these plates, which have so much puzzled us, are some form of screen or armor against the impact of meteorites?"

"By God!" said Keyes. "I believe you're right."

"And even more," continued Le Maistre. "They have either given their station an artificial gravity so huge as to make the assault of meteorites a positive danger—in which case the attention of our medical officers should be invited to the possibility that this is the source of their immunity from radiation disease—or they have never escaped from an immense theoretical error, the error of the bygone 1940s. They are still unaware that a meteorite can arrive at a station in space only with a speed determined by the mutual attraction of the objects——"

"Unless it's traveling on a direct collision course under

the attraction of some other body," corrected Keyes.

"Which in the case of a meteorite and a space station is practically null," finished Le Maistre. "Gentlemen, I am delighted with the kidnaping and questioning of Mr. Duruy. It has yielded us more information than the espionage service has been able to secure in two years."

General Gebhard's fingers played with the model of a rocket. "Pretty theoretical, isn't it, though?" he said.

"Not all of it, sir," said Keyes. "If those big plates on their station are armor against meteorites they can't have any great weight of armament aboard. Not as much as our station."

Duruy said suddenly, "Oh, one thing I forgot while they were questioning me. They asked me when I was going back, if that has any importance."

"Most decidedly it could have," said Le Maistre. "They know you are the calculator operator, and are aware that out people are frequently attacked by the radiation disease. What if they take the hazard of creating a situation —in Libya, for example—and launching torpedoes at a time when they believe our station is not at full efficiency? This is something we must consider, *mon général.*"

Gebhard pivoted round to face Fuller. "How soon can you get the relief rocket away?"

"It isn't fully provisioned yet. The parts for the new construction and the forty additional torpedoes are aboard, though. If I put an extra crew on the job, say five days."

"Make it in three. That's an order. Duruy."

"Yes, sir."

"You still stand reprimanded. On the other hand, you're going out there on a perilous mission. You're probably the only man in the world today who can prevent a war developing out of the current political situation, because the Russians know you're too good. I want to wish you the best of luck."

IV

☐ Sprawled out in the desert, the *Goddard* looked gigantic, even beside the upthrust of the mountains. She had an odd resemblance to a grinning shark, tilted up at an angle, with the tall spider web of scaffolding beneath her nose, the huge swept-back wings at the sides, the tiny dorsal fin at her back, and the open hatches beneath the forward end, where supplies were being hoisted in.

"I didn't know——" began Duruy, but what it was he didn't know was cut off by a roar of sound, as one of the huge jet engines in the wings, that would take them up to the point where the rocket drive assumed responsibility, was cut in for a test.

The roar died. "Okay on Number Four, Jake," megaphoned someone from aloft.

"What did you say?" asked Captain Keenan.

"That the situation was that serious."

"You don't have to believe it is. Old Smalley tries to give everyone the dark blue collywobbles. It makes him feel that a briefing officer is really important, instead of being just a mouthpiece for the brass."

"Mmmm," said Duruy. "Still, they pulled you in from the Antarctic project. And Dr. Halvorsson—that research he was doing on radio-biology was pretty important. Not to mention my humble self. I ought to be designing calculators, not just running them. They had me working on a fully automatic, and now that will have to be laid aside."

Keenan took off his cap and ran a hand through grizzled graying hair. "Listen, son," he said. "On the day you get that fully automatic calculator I'll turn in my pilot's license. How are you going to persuade it to react when the 'Data insufficient' panel flashes up?"

"The same way you or I would," said Duruy stubbornly. "After all, the electronic reaction is faster than the human. And it should be possible to build relays that will analyze the data and discover the point at which the insufficiency appears."

"And then to have an inspiration about rephrasing the problem, the way you do, I suppose?" said Keenan.

"I don't know about the inspiration," said Duruy. "But the interceptors are fully automatic, aren't they? And theoretically, that ought to be the harder problem, with the first part of their run being made in air."

"Wonder if they'll ever get an interceptor that will stop a torpedo from space the way they catch intercontinental rockets fired from the ground?" said the captain. "I can remember the time when I didn't think it was possible they could do that. It took the explosion over Greenland to convince me."

A power unit towing a train of little trucks loaded with cases gave an ear-piercing skreawk and both men jumped aside. The announcement speaker bellowed: "Hear this: all members of the *Goddard's* crew report to Administration. All members of the *Goddard's* crew report to Administration."

"That means us," said Duruy. "I wonder what they want now."

"Can't imagine," said Keenan, falling into step beside him. "Something new in the line of red tape, doubtless."

The Administration Building, with its double steel shutter doors that protected the contents against the blast of take-offs, was before them, the sentry smartly presenting arms to Keenan. Most of the other fourteen members of the crew were already in the lounge, smoking, talking, drinking Coke instead of the more powerful liquids forbidden before a trip outside the atmosphere. Major Smalley, the briefing officer, a small fussy man with a pince-nez, trotted around among them in an agitated manner. As the last crewmen came in he raised a hand for silence.

"In view of the international situation," he said, "the high command has made a regulation that after crew members have been briefed no outgoing mail will be accepted from them unless placed in an unsealed envelope for censorship before being dispatched. All such letters will be mailed after you leave. Sorry not to have mentioned it before, and I am sure you will all understand."

There was a buzz of talk. Duruy got up and slid over to one of the writing desks. He hadn't tried to write to Tina during the hectic five days that had followed his rescue and the quick flight from Rio to White Sands, but now he thought he would, even though he didn't have any address for her. A letter in care of the Guycochéas ought to reach her sometime, and would let her know that, whatever the difficulties, he wasn't going to give up on the hope of seeing her again.

The pen was scratchy and the paper not of the best quality. As he finished the note and tucked it in the envelope he saw Dr. Halvorsson, one of the two medics allotted to the crew, standing beside him.

"Busy?" he asked.

"Not particularly," said Duruy. "Want something?"

"Just a question or two about a possible line of research. I understand that we specialists not connected with the running departments have a good deal of free time out there."

"I don't know how much free time I'll have after they build the extension to the station and start setting up the new torpedoes. I'll have to work out courses for several targets on them. But up to that time I'll be fairly free, I imagine. Except that—but go on."

The doctor was large and blond, with a meditative face. "I've been wondering," he said, "why it wouldn't be possible to work out some kind of a small communication rocket that would enable written messages to be carried to and from the station. This method of hanging out signals to be picked up by radar is thoroughly unsatisfactory. Not only are they subject to decoding, especially since they have to be so brief, but they don't really convey the information we need. Look at that last communication—'Grave danger, two-fifties.' I know they're in trouble out there, but I haven't the least idea how many of them or what stage the disease is in. It makes a lot of difference with regard to what measures I prepare to take."

Duruy said, "I agree that it's a damned shame the radio people can't find any way of getting through the Heavyside layer without hopelessly garbling everything they send, but I'm not sure message rockets would be the answer. The calculation for getting them there in either direction would be awfully arduous."

"Not more than for the torpedoes, would it?"

"Considerably. In firing a torpedo, you want an impact at the end of the run, a big smash. A message rocket would have to arrive in shape to deliver the message, so velocity would have to be considered, which would mean the addition of another major factor. And there's one more thing: in a war situation, which is just when they'd want messages the most, the enemy could put up interceptors after the slow-moving messengers. There's no way of concealing the fact that something is leaving a station in space."

Dr. Halvorsson's face showed disappointment. "I had hoped——"

Duruy went on, "And I'm not sure I could work out

the problem out there, anyway. You know about the effect of weightlessness on intellectual activity?"

"Yes, I'm familiar with that. As a matter of fact Dr. Montelius is going out to take up that very matter. He's a specialist in psychosomatic questions, you know. I only hope that the reaction doesn't prove inhibiting on his own activities. Well, I think I'll try to get in a nap. If they have some bad cases out there, there'll be precious little sleep for me for some time to come."

Duruy rose with him, hunted up Major Smalley to give him the letter, then wandered to the door. Out there the supplies seemed to be nearly all aboard. Only one hatch was still working, and a pair of tank trucks had swung in under one of the *Goddard's* wings to pump fuel for her jet engines through elephant-trunklike hoses. It would be about midnight when they took off to catch up with Project Excelsior in its slow revolution over and over the earth, past the Rockies, Alaska, and so over the top of the world across European Russia. He recalled how the tip of the Black Sea had looked, so very unlike the map; when he first saw it, it must have been about dawn down there, so that the land looked light and the water dark.

A couple of hours to kill. He wandered back into the lounge, got a cup of coffee and a magazine, and settled himself to wait, but that wasn't much good either. He kept thinking about Tina and whether his letter would reach her, and what she would say or do if it did. He got up to go over to the recreation center, then remembered that was off limits since he had been briefed, and ended by going out to watch the loading until the announcer called crew members into Administration again to put on their acceleration suits.

One of the mechanics and the new torpedo machinist were helping each other into the clumsy, foam-rubber-lined garments that made a man look like a collection of animated balloons. The latter's name was Grandissi, Duruy recalled, a small, dark man who looked as Italian as his name sounded, and whom Duruy did not particularly like.

He was chattering energetically with his companion as they fitted the parts of the suit together. "Look," he said. "Ten million dollars is a lot of money to spend sending us up there, just so we can threaten those Russians. That would buy an awful lot of housing."

"Ah, g'wan," said the mechanic. "They oughta build three more stations like the one we got. Then maybe those guys would lay off us."

"Then the Russians would only build more stations themselves. All they want is we should lay off them. The way it is now, the country is getting so loaded up with expense for armaments that they have to have a war to protect the investment."

"I don't get that," said the mechanic. "You're just nuts."

Grandissi appealed. "Isn't that right, Mr. Duruy? That all these armaments could bring on a depression."

Duruy said, "I don't know. Economics isn't my line. I doubt that it's ever happened in practice, in spite of what the early Marxists used to say, and I think we're a long way from the breakdown point when the Allied governments can't afford to build but one ship to service the station. I can't figure out why Congress beat the appropriation bill for the second *Goddard*."

"It's because they won't tax the big corporations enough," said Grandissi. "They got too much voice in the government."

Duruy snapped shut the headpiece of his acceleration suit. It annoyed him to hear arguments that ran off into generalizations like this, and he wanted to test the internal air pressure anyway. It was okay. He raised an arm and signaled to one of the line crew, who was coming down the alley of the dressing room, pushing one of the little carts in which the suited members of the crew would be carried out to the big rocket.

He could see but not hear the man call for a helper, and was lifted aboard the cart, where he fixed his hand tools to the railing. It was completely dark outside; Duruy was trundled down an avenue of floodlight to a position beneath one of the hatches of the *Goddard*, where a platform elevator reached down long arms to draw him into the interior of the ship. Inside, he let down the wheels of his suit, fixed the hand tools to the guide rail, and trundled rapidly along into the passenger compartment, where five or six men were already in the deeply cushioned seats.

Hose connection to the ship's air supply—okay. He hooked in the phone connection and said, "Duruy, testing phone."

"How do you do, Duruy?" said a voice he recognized as that of Dr. Montelius. "Montelius speaking."

"Fine as silk, so far," said Duruy. "They've improved these suits a lot since the first time I went out, though."

"Had to——" began the doctor, but a voice cut in: "Clear the general circuit for tests, please. Long speaking."

"Okay, Captain," came the doctor's voice, and then: "Eggersfeld, mechanic first, testing phone. Do you hear me?"

"You are coming through okay, Eggersfeld," said the voice of Captain Long, the co-pilot. "Do you hear me?"

"I hear you. Eggersfeld out."

The reports went on. Presently a new voice cut in: "Keenan speaking. I have cut exterior connections. We have one minute to go unless someone has a necessary adjustment. Report if you have." A silence. "Forty-five seconds, forty, thirty-five, thirty . . ."

The count reached its end and the *Goddard* began to

shake violently, though the roar of the jet engines was muted to a gentle purring. In the carefully insulated suits and even more carefully insulated seats there was no sensation of pressure at the take-off, only a smoothing out of the vibration. Duruy knew they were rushing up into the night at a speed beyond that of sound, but from where he lay the view panels of the control room were not visible.

"Stand by," came Keenan's voice over the phone, and with a roar the rocket engine cut in. Duruy felt himself jerked back with a weight four times that he had on earth, and felt the air machine labor to help him breathe. "Jeez!" came a strangled voice over the phone; "Atch!" came another, and then Keenan's voice, slowed by the effort it cost him to speak: "Silence—on—the—main—circuit."

He was not trying to keep track of time, but it seemed like an hour before the captain cut back in with "Stand by," and a second later the vibrating blast of the rocket was missing from the hull. Duruy bounced upward; the huge metal encasement in which he had barely been able to lift an arm while on earth was abruptly as light as a pair of swimmer's trunks, and his stomach felt as though it were being wrenched round and round by a pair of gigantic hands. There wasn't any up or down any more; clinging cautiously to the guide rail with one hand, he reached the other up, cut the pressure air supply, and unscrewed his headpiece.

The cabin presented the usual appearance of such a place a minute or two after rocket drive is cut. Up against the ceiling a sausagelike figure was making vague swimming motions, the startled face of the navigator visible through the headpiece. Back in the corner one of the mechanics had his headpiece off and was being violently sick into one of the vessels provided for the purpose. Dr. Halvorsson had taken off his armpieces and was fishing in the cabinet for the little bottles of brandy laced with pepsin with which the qualms of the crew would be somewhat quieted.

Captain Long's voice said, "See that. No, over there. It's a big one. The Russkis must be sending up their relief ship too. Now I wonder what made them do it at just the time we're going out."

V

☐ A series of bumps and scrapings was transmitted through the *Goddard's* hull as the powered magnetic units maneuvered her across the hexagonal plates of the space station to the point where her exit hatches would correspond with the intakes of Project Excelsior.

Captain Keenan gazed from the control-room window at the three men in acceleration suits, wired together like Alpine climbers, who were skipping with awkward speed across the brilliantly lighted surface of the station. "What's the matter with them in there?" he said. "Don't they know the drag is likely to disturb the orbit if they don't make that hookup integral soon? Only three men on the job!"

Dr. Halvorsson said, "I don't like to sound grim, Captain, but if the station's message bears one interpretation, it could mean that they only have three men fit for duty."

"Out of sixteen?" Keenan looked incredulous. "How will they get the *Goddard* back to White Sands?"

"Not my problem." The doctor shrugged. "I will say, though, that if men are going to do much work outside the station and exposed to the full force of the cosmic rays, they need more rapid relief than we're providing for this crew."

"That's just the trouble," Keenan said. "The political side never understands what we're up against. Build the station bigger, they say, and triple its torpedo capacity.

Then because we say we have to have another *Goddard* in a hurry we're stupid militarists who don't even know our own business."

Long handed himself along the guide rail, his curly hair bouncing. "That's not altogether fair to Congress, though, is it, Captain? After all, they were ready to go ahead, when the European members of the alliance refused to meet their share of the bills."

"Damned fools," growled Keenan.

"Oh, I don't know," said Dr. Montelius, who was floating just behind Keenan. "After all, it's a question of ideals. They thought the world was free of atomic wars for good when the interceptors were invented and now we come along with this space station, and the show starts all over again. There's a certain amount of reasonableness in their claim that we ought to accept the Russian offer to keep the space stations unarmed."

"The Russians would never keep the agreement, and you ought to know it," said Keenan. "There, they've just about got it."

He faced round toward the cabin. "Attention! Everybody tighten up your suits and use the contained air supply. There's sometimes an air leak when these joints are fitted together. And hook in on the main phone circuit."

There was a mild bustling in the cabin as the crew members got back into the headpieces they had discarded and pulled themselves into positions where they could plug in. When Duruy hooked his own line into the circuit, communication had already been established between ship and station.

"—ready," Keenan's voice was saying. "Open her up."

Even over the phones the grind of gears was audible as a section of the station's outer wall swung inward, taking with it a similar section of the *Goddard's* hull, and leaving directly over Duruy's head a yawning passage which ended in another door.

"Okay, Long," said Keenan. "You go first."

The co-pilot stepped down from the control cabin with an odd effect of mincing, balanced himself delicately in the center of the main cabin, and leaped, with arms stretched overhead. He floated gently upward through the gap.

Keenan said, "Watch how he did it, you people here for the first time, and don't give it too hard a push or you're liable to ram your head against that door on the far side. I'll have Long and someone else wait there to catch you, but try to take it easy. Remember, you only weigh a couple of pounds out here. All right, Etchardy, you're next."

The navigator took Long's place, then came Duruy, and one by one the others, Keenan himself last of all. There were one or two minor accidents, but no damage; Keenan braced himself, swung the outer hatch shut, and turned to the inner one. It opened into a long compartment with the usual guide rails at top, sides, and bottom, in which a man with a shock of red hair and a lightweight summer uniform appeared to be hanging upside down. As the newcomers began to take off headpieces he reversed himself quickly, and shook hands with Keenan.

"My God, but I'm glad to see you," he said. "We're in terrible shape here. I've only got four men fully fit, and both of my medics are gone. We had to stop work on the extension."

"Two-fifties?" queried Keenan.

"Unless it's some other epidemic giving the same symptoms." He saw Halvorsson emerge from his headpiece. "Oh, hello, Doctor. I couldn't be more glad to see you if you were an angel from heaven. Is there anything you can do for my people?"

Halvorsson shook his head. "Not very much, short of hospitalization back on earth where they won't be getting additional doses of radiation every day. I can arrest things for a couple of days, but that's as far as we've got."

The red-haired man shook his head. "We thought you

might have hit something in six months. I knew you were working on it."

Keenan turned around and faced the little group. "You will follow Captain O'Brien and myself," he said. "He will call off the quarters for each man as we go down the passage. You have already been assigned to watches. Those belonging to Section One will go on duty first" —he looked at his watch—"half an hour from now. That will give everyone a chance to get out of his acceleration suit and to stow his personal luggage. Section Two, off duty until zero six hundred, then all hands except cooks on unloading detail until eighteen hundred, when Section One falls out. Any questions?"

One of the mechanics raised a hand. "Yes, Captain. What good are cooks when we can't keep down anything we eat?"

There was a mild laugh and the procession started down the corridor of the compartment, each man falling out as his name was called and passing through one of the oval, rubber-lined doors into the cubicle that was to be his home for the next months. Duruy found his in corridor A-5, close to the "top" of the station as seen from the earth and near the big calculating machine that was his special care, the cabin that had been occupied by his opposite number of the other section during his previous visit. Even if the station had grown bigger in the meantime, this hadn't changed much. There were the same lights, the same table bolted to one wall, with the chair beneath it, also bolted in place, so that you always banged your knees getting in it to work. There was the same tubular bed let into the wall, the same controls for air and heat.

He was due on duty. He crawled out of the acceleration suit, dumped it in a locker, picked a pair of magnetized shoes out of another, and started down the corridor to the calculating room. Someone had spilled a drop of water; it floated past him, disturbed by the small breeze of his passage, like a tiny iridescent balloon, and once more he found himself thinking of Tina and how she would react to a place like this.

The door of the calculating room was locked. He rapped, and the speaker beside the door said in a tinny voice, "Who is it?"

"Duruy, new crew, relieving you."

"Oh."

There was a click, the door gave to his touch, and he was in the familiar calculating room with its banks of tubes and panels. The man sitting at the pipe-organlike board said, "Papers, please."

Duruy produced them, noticing that the other had lost some of his hair, and there was a red skin infection running across his scalp. The man glanced over the papers, handed them back, stuck out his hand, and said in a toneless voice, "I'm Scott. Glad to have you aboard."

"Glad to be aboard," said Duruy. "What's the matter? Have you been mixing up with the two-fifties too?"

"Some. I'm not as bad as some of the mechanics, though. One of them went blind yesterday, and two of them are dead."

"Good God! Why the epidemic?"

"When the mechanics started to go down, all of us had to turn to and try to work outside on building the extension for the new torpedoes. O'Brien ordered it, the bastard." His face contorted suddenly. "He's the one that makes us keep Calculation locked, too. Apparently afraid there might be a Russian agent aboard. Tell me, is the situation back there on earth as tight as it was when we left?"

"It's worse. The Chicago Cubs are leading the league."

Scott had only a small smile for this crack. Now that one looked at him closely, he did have the appearance of a thoroughly sick man. Duruy went on. "I'm not violating my confidence when I tell you that General Gebhard said, just before we left, that this station is about the only thing that can prevent a war."

"They'd better send out their reliefs faster then," said Scott. "How are they coming with the second space rocket?"

"Hardly at all. I think there's still some construction going on on it, but it's at least a year and a half away, and when the European members of the alliance refused to pay any more toward its completion, Congress voted down the appropriation to pay for it ourselves."

"They must be crazy down there. All right, relieve me, will you? I need to get some sleep. The navigator can't get out of his bunk, and I've been on duty for sixteen hours."

"I relieve you."

Scott shuffled out with the peculiar dragging step of a man hard hit by the dreaded radiation disease. Duruy shuddered a little as he sat down and began to check over the data sheets. There were tubes for thirty-one torpedoes instead of the twenty-four he had known, but no lines of flight had been calculated for any of them yet, apparently because the torpedoes themselves were still aboard the *Goddard* being brought out this trip. Number One's sheet still bore the calculations he had made on his first trip, for a flight to Moscow if fired any time between thirteen-thirty and fourteen twenty-two, but a firm hand had annotated it for earlier firing if the station were given a one-degree change of orbit. Number Two, Sevastopol or Leningrad, that was his basic calculation, too, but some of the figures had been changed at two places beyond the decimal point. He'd have to recheck that one. Number Three, Number Four . . .

The order sheet was signed "O'Brien" and bore instructions for Number Twenty-five—calculate to run a spiral orbit and strike some place called Uralskoi. He didn't even know where it was, and those spiral orbits were dangerous; unless the torpedo were released at precisely the right moment and on precisely the right bearing, it might leave the solar system altogether or treat the dusty deserts of Mars to a taste of atomic bombing. Matter of split-second timing—and also of chess-player skill in handling the calculator. He noticed that Scott hadn't even begun on the problem, probably too hard hit by either the effect of weightlessness or the two-fifties. He'd have to check with Keenan and see whether the skipper really thought that spiral orbit necessary, though as a general rule the orders left by one captain were carried through by his relief.

Someone knocked. "Come in," called Duruy and then remembered that he hadn't locked up after Scott left.

It was Etchardy, the navigator, who would be his relief on the calculator when the other section was on duty, a blond with a thin face and a look of youthfulness. "My stomach was so upset I couldn't sleep," he said, "so I thought I'd case the joint and get acquainted."

"Sit down," said Duruy. "What's everybody doing?"

"Unloading. I don't think I'm going to get used to seeing one man walk off with a case that weighs eight or nine hundred pounds on earth and has to be handled with a crane." He surveyed the front of the machine with interest. "Where do the data sheets live?"

"Right here. Have you looked over your observatory yet?"

"Oh yes. It's a little lulu. Whoever built this station was on the ball. But the man I'm relieving got way behind in his work, and I've got to do a recalculation on some of the planetoids. He's lost track of Hermes, and Albert isn't even on the sheets, which isn't so good when you consider that the damned hunk of rock weighs three billion tons and has an orbit so irregular that it has to be recalculated practically every Friday. I wouldn't want to find us on a collision course."

"If you do, notify me, and we'll feed Albert a torpedo," said Duruy, and both laughed slightly.

Etchardy stirred his feet as though he had something on his mind, and then said, "Tell me, what do you think of our team?"

"Most of them seem all right to me. The skipper's a good, hard solid citizen of a rocket pilot, pretty competent; I've known him for a while."

"I wasn't thinking of him," said Etchardy.

"Well, the mechs seem the usual lot. Dr. Halvorsson is a very distinguished scientist, rather on the stiff side, and I rather like Long."

"So do I. I've been with him through training, and he's all right, even if he did spend every evening out with a different babe. He's going to find it lonely out here. But I wasn't thinking of him. What do you think of our good friend Dr. Montelius?"

"The psychosomatic specialist?" said Duruy. "Well——"

"He's Germany's gift to Project Excelsior. Came from there originally, you know, even though he hasn't a trace of an accent."

"Oh," said Duruy. "That might explain it."

"What?"

"When we were coming in he was giving a lecture on how he thought the European members of the alliance were right in not paying for another service ship. We ought to accept the Russian offer to disarm both stations and make them scientific laboratories."

Etchardy rubbed his chin. "That's what I mean. I don't like the way the guy thinks."

"But if he's German it's probably all right. I know quite a lot of them. They go off into philosophical abstractions at a moment's notice, or even without notice, but an order's an order and when they have a job to do they do it without question."

"Maybe, but——"

The intercom in the wall buzzed sharply. "Duruy, Calculation," said Duruy, throwing the switch and putting his face close to it.

"Captain Keenan requests you will come to his cabin."

"Okay."

Etchardy got up. "See you later. You relieve me here at fourteen hundred?"

VI

☐ The captain's face was grave as Duruy stepped into his cabin, and he got up to snap the lock. "Sit down, Lambert," he said.

"What's up?"

"This: I know you've had your general briefing like the rest of us, and you're pretty well up with the general situation. But I was given a special briefing before we left, with instructions not to say anything about it till we got out here, and then to be careful who I spoke to. And I'm telling you about it because you're the only member of the crew who's been out here before, and I'm sure of you.

"Thanks."

"Colonel le Maistre thinks there is reason to believe we may have a Russian agent in the crew."

"Good God! What's the matter with Security? Can't they check people any more?"

Keenan shook his head. "They've checked everyone aboard till they're blue in the face. Some of them are even last-minute replacements of people who were previously scheduled to come. That doesn't make any difference. We have our own agents in Russia, you know, and they came through recently with a report that the boys in the Kremlin were feeling pretty happy over having planted someone here. We don't know how, or who it is or anything, but that's the reason O'Brien set up the order that Calculation was to admit no one without a Top Secret pass."

"I see," said Duruy. "That could be rough, all right. But what do you want me to do? Play being Sherlock Holmes?"

"No, that's about the last thing I want you to do. Le Maistre's a pretty hot Sherlock himself, you know. When he got that report he immediately started figuring out what an agent could do up here. He'd be after information, for one thing, but that wouldn't do him much good, because he'd have no way of communicating it until he got back to earth."

"Dr. Halvorsson was asking me if I couldn't work out the calculations for the delivery of messages by small rockets," said Duruy thoughtfully.

"I don't think that puts the finger on Halvorsson. You'd still be in control of the rockets. Neither would Le Maistre think so. His line of reasoning is that an agent could hardly sabotage the station itself, except maybe to destroy our gear for changing the orbit. That wouldn't matter; our orbit as it stands will let us bomb anything important the Russians have. And he could hardly sabotage the torpedo rooms. There are too many of them and he'd be caught before he half finished the job. But the calculator is the key of the whole business. Without that, we're just a hunk of hardware floating around up here in the sky."

"I see. So you want me to watch it with more than human care."

Keenan's face did not relax. "More than that. I want you to watch yourself too. The calculator isn't much use without you. Etchardy's a good man, and with the data sheets he could fire some shots in an emergency, but not enough to get decisive results. And Le Maistre thinks that an agent would figure that the calculator would be under careful guard and concentrate on disabling the operator."

Duruy smiled ruefully. "Well, I suppose it's no worse than being one of those South American presidents they're always trying to assassinate. What do I do?"

"I've worked out a program. There aren't enough of us for me to give you a bodyguard, and anyway, the bodyguard might turn out to be the wrong man, so you'll just have to be careful. I'm having your gear moved into the cabin next to mine here, which Long should be occupying, and moving him down one. That way, there'll always be one of us in the next cabin when you're off duty. Don't open your door except to one of us, and whichever one it is will accompany you along the corridor to where you want to go. When you're off duty and in the main cabin, don't let yourself be left alone with one man. Don't take any meals alone, and when you do eat, wait till somebody else has tasted some of it first."

"You make me sound like a piece of bric-a-brac. Can I play cards with the big boys, Teacher?"

"If you're careful." Keenan was still not giving an inch. He stood up. "The regime goes into effect now, as an order. I'll walk down to Calculation with you and pick you up there when you come off duty."

They passed one or two men snaking boxes along the corridor. As Duruy stuck his key in the lock of the calculation compartment Keenan said, "Oh yes. Just before I got aboard the *Goddard*, Captain Bennett-Drax handed me this to give to you. Been so busy I forgot it before. This whole business may not be serious, so cheer up. 'By."

He waved a hand and the door closed. Duruy sat down in his calculator's chair and tore open a long envelope addressed to him in Bennett-Drax's flowing English hand. There were two papers inside, and Duruy's heart gave a dreadful jump as he saw one of them was the farewell letter he had written to Tina, still in its envelope and open. The other was another letter:

DEAR LAMBERT:

I hate to write this to you, especially in view of the contents of the enclosed, which has been handed to me for censorship; but I don't think it should be mailed, even to an address where it will probably not reach her. Because, Lambert, we have the best of evidence for believing that Tina Castelhoso is not only a Russian agent but is identical with Tatiana Vsevolod, who is one of their best rocket technicians. You probably aren't going to believe this, or just take it for the work of an interfering busybody, so I'll tell you that I've been on the radiophone with Rolim of the Segrêda most of the morning. They have traced her back from introduction to introduction until they did find someone who met her at Foz de Igussý in Paraná, but even then she didn't have any background, just plenty of money and plenty of time. And that was just about the date when you received your leave to take a vacation in Rio.

In the other direction, she chartered a small plane which left Rio for Montevideo the night you were kidnaped. At Monte she booked a seat on the Línea Aérea Uruguayana plane for Buenos Aires, giving the name Valdes, but apparently never occupied it. That is, we lose touch with her completely, which isn't surprising, as the Uruguayan police weren't looking for anything. Also her physical description checks almost exactly with that we have from our agents in Russia of Tatiana Vsevolod.

Now I realize that none of these items is conclusive by itself; in undercover work almost nothing ever is. Agents are trained to leave a trail of inconclusiveness. But the whole thing put together, with the fact that you were going out to Petropolis to meet her that night —and don't tell me you weren't, even if you won't confess it—makes it about as certain as anything can be in this business that she was sent out to pump you or, failing that, draw you into the kind of trap you fell into.

Lambert, I'm not blaming you. I know you're pretty much gone on the girl and, it's evident from your letter, very sincerely. And I think she's gone on you, too, in the same way. You told me she never talked to you about your work or the station, and it's perfectly clear that nobody but she could have called me up that night with the warning that you weren't to go to Petropolis after all. In other words, she threw down her bosses and took the chance on being liquidated for your sake.

I only hope they didn't liquidate her, and believe me, I wish we lived in the kind of world where two people in love could afford to forget international boundaries. But you can see why I'm sending this letter back and not passing it through.

Yours,
Peter J. B. Bennet-Drax

Duruy let the letter slip from his hand. It hung there in the weightless atmosphere of the space station, vibrating gently above his knees. The annunciator system bell clanged three times, and a voice announced:

"Stand by for entering eclipse phase! Stand by for entering eclipse phase! Prepare to turn on all heaters in two minutes."

In the next couple of days Duruy began to learn something about his fellow crew members of Project Excelsior, though not enough to provide ground for a definite suspicion of any one of them as a possible Russian agent. Etchardy was a bridge player of the first class, peculiarly precise in his bidding; with help he ought to make a good calculator operator himself someday. Captain Keenan, on the other hand, had a tendency to stick to regulations. He played a rather wooden game of bridge and drove his crew mercilessly at the task of getting the *Goddard* unloaded and the stretcher cases among the relieved crew aboard.

Dr. Halvorsson was quiet and calm. He spent little time in the main cabin where meals were taken and a good deal with his patients or in the medical laboratory, complaining that he had to learn his analytical techniques all over again in a place where there was no gravity to carry liquids through the apparatus. The communicator was named MacCartney; he came from Canada and had an endless fund of stories, which he told on all occasions.

The cook in Duruy's section was a big, burly man from the deep South, but after the second day it became clear that he was one of the unfortunates who could never overcome space sickness, and Dr. Montelius recommended that he be sent back with the *Goddard*. Grandissi, the little torpedo machinist, turned out to be a highly acceptable substitute, though he grumbled about being overworked.

Duruy himself felt lonely, depressed, and out of touch with the rest. They had trained together as a group and developed certain intimacies and references to common experiences which he knew nothing about. It might be that the thought of Tina lay like a dead weight on his mind, or it might be just that old effect of weightlessness creeping up on him quicker this time, inhibiting not only intellectual activity but the desire to have any intellectual activity.

He said as much to Keenan the day after the *Goddard* took off in a brief flare of flame and left them alone in space, while they were sitting in the captain's cabin, celebrating the occasion by sipping manhattan cocktails from plastic containers through straws. "It may be just that I'm getting old, but I'm not sure I'm up to the racket for any long period any more. I hope that they hurry up with that training program and get some of the new boys out here, like Norcross or that Greek kid from California."

Keenan carefully hung his drink in the air in front of him. "In the report going back I've recommended in the strongest terms I can that they get a relief crew out here in half the usual time," he said. "And Dr. Halvorsson has made that double. We can't have another crew going to pieces the way O'Brien's did. Of course it's that new construction work on the outside of the station that does it, exposing the men to unshielded cosmic radiation for long periods. But I can't skimp on that. The whole value of the station lies in building it up to double the old capacity. Besides, it's an order."

"It seems to me," said Duruy, "that O'Brien was a little —injudicious in putting everybody aboard onto construction, even his calculator. Scott was in terrible shape."

"What else could he do? He had to get the work done, and from his account the two-fifties hit the gang rather suddenly. Bad luck losing both his medics the first crack, though. They might have warned him in time to take a slowdown. I'm going to take good care of Halvorsson and see that nothing like that happens to him. Besides, I believe he's got more on the ball than either of the men O'Brien had."

"Well, anyway, I'll be glad when a relief shows up for me."

Keenan gave a wry smile and took a sip of his repossessed drink. "That's the bad news for you, Lambert. It won't. You'll have to stay over the next trip and break in the new man."

"What!" Duruy felt the lines of strain come into his face.

"Figure it out for yourself. Scott will be under treatment for months, and there's no one else with the necessary experience. It'll be all right, though. I'll keep you well inside and away from the construction work."

Duruy said, "It seems a damn shame they can't send a couple of calculators out here and train them on the job."

"Don't kick about conditions. You know as well as I do that the station will hold only so many people. Every time one more is added, another has to be dropped from somewhere." He held up his fingers to enumerate. "You've got to have two shifts. You can't sacrifice the torpedo machinist, or the communicator, or the medic, or the commander, or the cook. The rest are the mechanics for new construction. And when you try to double up on any of the functions you get fatigue and a higher susceptibility to the two-fifties."

"All the same——"

"All the same, they're trying to do something about it. That's one of the reasons for the extension of the station. It's just our hard luck to have to be the pioneers."

There was a rap at the door. "Who is it?" asked Keenan.

"MacCartney, sir."

"Come along in. Got a message?"

The communicator had a code book in his hand. Duruy noticed that his face seemed unusually pale beneath its garment of freckles, and that he saluted formally, which he didn't usually do. "We started coming in on White Sands about an hour ago," he said, "and I noticed they were burning flash powder for us to use our radar. I tuned it in, and the best I can get out of it is KGLF."

He handed the code book to Keenan, and Duruy, bending over, followed the captain's finger along the line. It read:

KGLF—SERVICE SHIP HAS CRASHED

"Of course, it may not be true," said MacCartney. "I'm putting out the code signs for confirmation, and the next time we go over, about five days from now, I may get another reading. But as of now, it looks as though we're stuck with it."

VII

☐ Captain Keenan held up his hand. "I have called this meeting," he said, "because I want everyone to understand the exact situation and stop jabbering about it among yourselves. Also to see whether some of you can't tear those gigantic intellects away from the contemplation of bridge and acey-deucy long enough to give a little thought to the problems of the station. If anybody has any bright ideas, this is the occasion to produce them."

He stopped and looked around. In the group packed into the main cabin there was no sound but the clearing of throats. "All right," said Keenan. "I want you all to understand at the start that this isn't any debating club. I'm captain of this station and I intend to remain so and give my own orders. This is a session for your own information. But I will listen to anything you have to say. Now I'm going to have Lieutenant MacCartney describe the result of his communication with White Sands first. Go ahead, Mac, I release you from the regs on messages."

"We-ell," began the communicator slowly. His voice had a pleasant slight burr of Scots. "It's not so easy, you see, carrying on a conversation when you can make only one remark in every five days, six hours, and fourteen minutes. It reminds me of a trapper up in the Temagami, named MacGregor——"

"We've heard that one," said someone.

"Have you now?" said MacCartney, unruffled. "I've been wondering what happened to a group that had heard all each other's stories, and now I'm thinking I know; they get downright impolite. As I was saying, it's not so easy. White Sands has to put out its radar-reflecting panels and we pick up the message as we go past, meanwhile sending one of our own. Now, you see, those messages are limited to four characters, and we interpret them through the code book. But the code book doesn't cover the situation we're in or anything very like it, so we have to feel our way along, and about half the time one or the other of us doesn't quite understand."

Dr. Halvorsson raised a hand and MacCartney beckoned him to go ahead. "Beg pardon, Lieutenant," said the doctor, "but wouldn't it be possible to spell out what you wanted to say in clear, even at the rate of four letters a time?"

"It would be possible, but not very desirable," said MacCartney judiciously. "We do not know how many radar stations the Russians have down there on earth, watching every signal we make, but we can be sure they have some. And as for White Sands signaling us in this way, there's that brute of a Russian station floating up there that would pick them up too."

Keenan said, "There's one thing you want to remember, too, Doctor. We know how much of a jam we're in, and down there, White Sands does too. But we don't know that the Russians know anything about it; they may not even be aware that the *Goddard* crashed. And if we don't let them find out we'll be a lot better off."

"I will continue," said MacCartney. "In the two months since we arrived here I have gathered enough to be more than medium sure that the *Goddard* crashed because of the poor physical condition of the crew that went home in her, and that it will be something like seven months more before she is repaired sufficiently to make a flight. There was something in one of the messages about a

'Number Two,' so I would take it that they have decided to go ahead with the second service ship."

"But she was more than a year away and work was stopped on her!" protested Long.

"That I know," said MacCartney. "I am telling you what I have learned."

Dr. Montelius raised a hand. "Is there any chance that the international situation down there has improved enough so they could borrow a service ship from the Russians?"

MacCartney glanced at Keenan, who nodded. "The chances are very poor, very poor," said the lieutenant. "One of the messages was an order to continue building —in answer to one from the captain here, asking if he should belay."

Keenan stood up again. "All right, men, there it is. We can't reasonably expect relief for something like seven months. Now, Grey, will you tell us the situation on supplies?"

The chief steward spoke. "We're in pretty good shape for that amount of time. Got all the air we need, and our losses in the locks when the men go out are small. As long as the solar-power motors hold out, and I see no reason why they should fall down, it will keep right on being purified. The water supply is okay too. In food, we may run short on a few things. The fresh eggs are about gone now, the milk won't last another three months nor the coffee another five, unless you stop using so much of it. The frozen vegetables will be gone in six months, even with economy, but we'll eat, all right."

"How about comic books?" called someone.

"You'd better read your Bible instead of such trash," said Grey, and there was a laugh. Everyone knew he was a Shouting Methodist.

Keenan said, "Dr. Montelius. Is there any reason to suppose that the shortage of fresh vegetables will produce deficiency diseases—scurvy, for example?"

"Not that I know of," said the doctor. "We're adequately supplied with all types of vitamins. It won't taste as good as though they came from the natural product, but there's no question about physical difficulties as a result."

"So far, so good, then," said Keenan. "Now I want all of you to stop worrying and discussing things like that. We have enough real difficulties not to anticipate imaginary ones. Now, Dr. Halvorsson, what's the position with regard to the two-fifties?"

"Not so favorable, I'm afraid," said the doctor. "The Geiger counts on the mechanics who are working outside have been running definitely high. I might almost say dangerously high. In my opinion these men should be kept in the interior of the ship, inside the compartments containing reserve air and water, which have a definite screening effect on the worst of the radiation."

"Are these men in any immediate danger?"

"None at all—in my opinion. I don't pretend to know very much about the type of radiation disease which you call the two-fifties. It appears to be a compound of several different types of illness. But if kept in the inner compartments these men will not acquire dangerous dosages."

"You can't do anything to delouse them—that is, reduce the quantity of radiation they have taken in already?"

"Not here, nor at present. You see, we all of us keep getting radiation right through the station all the time. As long as we're reasonably, or even slightly, protected it isn't enough to hurt, but it prevents any recovery. That can only be done on earth, under hospital conditions. It may be"—the doctor paused and made a little gesture—"that my colleague and I will succeed in solving the difficulties before we leave here. There's nothing inherently impossible in finding the answer. We just haven't done it yet."

"Thank you, Doctor. Now, has anybody any questions?"

There was a little shuffling in the room, a few words murmured from one man to another, but nobody had questions. Keenan raised his hand for attention again.

"Now, Doctor, I want to ask you one thing more. You realize, don't you, that what you have just said about keeping the men inside amounts to a recommendation that we violate our express orders to continue the work on the extension of the station—orders which have been repeated since we were marooned here?"

Halvorsson's face became slightly pinker. "I can't help that. You asked me for an opinion and I gave it. I'm a doctor, not an expert on international politics."

"I wish we knew more about the political side of the question," said Keenan. "But this much is perfectly clear. We pass over Russia at every revolution, beside which their station has us in full view, and there's one thing we can be damned sure of. They'll have every telescope that can be spared trained on us all the time, to see whether we're going ahead with the extension work, and the minute it stops, they'll know there's something wrong. I don't know what conditions down on earth are like just now, but if, knowing the conditions out here, they order us to go ahead building, they must be fairly tight. That's the situation. Now I'm going to call for volunteers from this crew to take the chance on doing the outside work. I'll cut the hours and the progress schedule, and I expect to lead any work parties myself, but that work *must go on*."

He stopped. Once more there was a murmur. Grey said, "Captain, I'll volunteer to help, but I'm awful clumsy with any tools except a skillet."

"I'll take you. Anybody else?"

Braggiotti, the assistant communicator, raised his hand. So did Duruy. So did a couple of others.

"Not you, Duruy. You know why, and I'm not even

going to explain to the rest. Howard, I won't accept you unless Dr. Halvorsson says you can stand it. Long, I won't accept you at all. This station has to have one commander who's in good health. That was what went wrong with O'Brien's crew. Etchardy, I'll take you for limited service, but only for short periods."

Dr. Halvorsson spoke up. "Captain, as long as this discussion is being held publicly, I'd like to make public a proposal. If the warhead were removed from one of the torpedoes, it seems to me that it would be easy to convert the space into a compartment that would hold several men. I think this should be done. In the event that we have really serious cases of radiation disease, the torpedo would then become an ambulance to take the affected persons back to base."

Keenan frowned. "All the torpedoes are directed against assigned targets on orders from the high command. I don't know that I'd feel justified in diverting any of them."

There was a murmur that spoke disagreement. Duruy said, "Captain, there has been a proposition similar to this up before. I don't think the idea is valid at all. In the first place, the torpedoes are built for such speeds that I doubt whether anyone could stand the acceleration, even in a suit. In the second, even if we did succeed in tinkering with the drive of one to bring the acceleration down to bearable proportions, I wouldn't care for the job of calculating a flight course and time that would bring it and its contents in safely. Those torpedoes are designed to fly on crash courses, not to land. There isn't any braking mechanism and only very limited means of control, once the thing is in flight. The whole idea is fantastic."

"I don't agree——" began Halvorsson, but Keenan held up a hand. "If it will satisfy you, Doctor, I'll go into the technical possibilities of your scheme, but I'm not sanguine about it. Now, has anyone else any ideas? Very well, dismiss; I'll put the new work and watch schedules on the annunciator as soon as I've worked them out. Come on, Lambert."

When they were in his cabin Keenan turned to Duruy frowningly. "What in the world was Halvorsson after with that crazy idea of his?" he said.

"I don't know. He did propose something like that just before we took off, but it's so obviously out of line this time that I wonder whether he isn't the Russian agent you're looking for."

"But what would his purpose be in putting up such a scheme if he is?"

Duruy scratched his head with one finger. "That's a little hard to figure. It might be just to undermine morale —though now that I think of it, I can't see how morale was much damaged, or would be. I guess the good doctor is just persistent in the pursuit of an idea. It makes him a good research worker. What about Montelius?"

"You mean you think he might be our man?"

"No, I haven't any direct suspicion of him," said Duruy slowly. "I just asked what about him."

"Nothing about him," said Keenan. "Or any other member of the crew, for that matter. Lambert, I've watched every man on this station until I feel as though my eyes were popping out, and I can't detect the slightest sign from a single man that he might be an agent. They've been going through wtih their duties like the hand-picked men they are. As for Montelius, he's been working on the theory that the mental slow-up up here traces to the lack of physical effort."

"The mechanics and torpedo machinists certainly put out enough physical effort."

"I know," said Keenan, "and it makes them sleepy, too. They have to have more rest. The whole thing is complicated, and I'm glad I'm not a doctor. But anyway, Montelius wants me to fit up a compartment in the new North 30 section, next to the torpedo-tube bank, as an exercise room."

"Wait a minute," said Duruy. "That doesn't sound too good to me. That North 30 section is outside the reserve water and air supplies, open to radiation. And it's just exactly work under radiation conditions that brings on the two-fifties."

"I know, but—no, Lambert, that's no more indicative than Halvorsson's proposition. Damn it, it's pretty rotten to have to be suspicious of the men you work with every day and depend on for help. To watch everything they do and consider what it might mean." The captain sat down gloomily, and Duruy turned to the door to go to his own cabin.

He almost collided with Etchardy, who came bouncing down the corridor with an expression of delight on his face.

"I've found Albert!" he almost shouted.

"That's nice," said Keenan, "but who is Albert?"

"Albert is asteroid Number 719, discovered by Palisa of Vienna in 1911. And he's damned important right at the present moment."

"All right. Why?"

"I'll explain. Albert was always pretty hot stuff, with a highly eccentric orbit that brought him pretty close to the earth at one end of it, and out near Jupiter's orbit at the other. Some time in the 1930s he got lost; that is, he didn't make his approach to earth on schedule. The astronomers figured that he got too close to Jupiter and Jupiter bullied him into a new orbit, but he was so small it was hardly worth running a search for him. Now look: when Blassingame was astronomer on this project he had to work out a course for Albert, because even though he's pretty small as a planet, he's plenty big enough to put a crimp in Project Excelsior. Blassingame didn't find him, and neither did Newman, because he came down with the two-fifties. But I've found him, and in a place that makes him just about the most important chunk of real estate in existence."

Etchardy paused, obviously enjoying the suspense he was producing.

"Go on," said Keenan, "give us the news."

Etchardy said, "Albert is on a direct collision course with the Russian station."

"What!" said Keenan, jumping up so rapidly that he went two feet off the floor and banged his head against the bulkhead. "Can they do anything about it?"

Duruy said, "I'm sure they can't. I was at a conference of the brass, just before take-off, and Colonel le Maistre was positive they didn't have any means of varying their orbit, the way we have."

"It ought to damage them some," said Keenan.

"It will wipe them out," said Etchardy. "Albert is moving a little faster than a torpedo. It's an incredible coincidence, a million-to-one chance, but the Russkis have just had the luck to hit that jackpot. I don't care how well they're protected; they can't stand Albert."

"Wonder what they'll do?" said Keenan. "Abandon ship probably, as soon as they can get their service ship up. Hmm, I don't see any reason for not telling the rest of the crew about this. It will cheer them up some. But I think we'll keep the news within the station. If we notify base, the Russians may be able to read our code, and it might give them a tip-off they don't have now. Is Albert visible from the earth where he is now?"

"If you look for him specially," said Etchardy. "There's no reason one should, though, except the nasty suspicion Blassingame had. He's still so far away that it will take something like six weeks before the blowup. But I'm pretty sure of my facts."

Duruy gave a wry smile. "Nice picture, isn't it?" he said. "One station about to die of the two-fifties and the other one about to blow up."

VIII

☐ Duruy said, "Who is it?"

"Halvorsson."

"Sorry, Doctor, can't let you in. Regulations."

"I'd like to see you about a rather private matter when you are off duty," came the voice through the door.

"Okay. Meet you in the main cabin."

"I said it was private."

Duruy didn't answer, pretending not to have heard, and reflecting that if he wanted to keep his reputation for sanity he'd have to get Keenan to relax the rule that he mustn't be alone with any other member of the crew. It was about as humiliating as any experience he remembered.

Nevertheless, the doctor was waiting at one of the tables in the main cabin when he came in, sipping coffee from a plastic ball. Halvorsson moved over to make room for him, glanced at the two mechanics who were playing acey-deucy in the opposite corner, tossing the dice in a box so they wouldn't fly clear across the compartment, and said in a low voice:

"This is a rather delicate matter. I'm approaching you on it because you seem more—intimate with the captain than anyone else."

"I think you overestimate, but go ahead."

"It's this matter of the construction. I've appealed to

him in every way I know to stop it, but he won't listen to me."

"Well, it's rough, but this is something close to war, and that's always rough," said Duruy. "The individual can't be considered."

"I am fully aware of that as a philosophical point," said Halvorsson. "But in the last three weeks things have reached so dangerous a stage that it isn't merely the individuals who are concerned, but the life of the station itself."

"How do you mean?"

"Braggiotti is showing definite lesions, and Jablotsky is dragging his feet. If the relief ship takes as long as they think I may not be able to save either of them."

"They're off construction duty now, aren't they?"

"Yes, but at the rate things are going, this crew will be in as bad shape as O'Brien's in another three months. And it will be another three months beyond that before we can hope for any relief. You see what I'm driving at."

"I do," said Duruy. "Haven't you presented this to Keenan?"

"This morning. He told me to mind my own business. You see, the worst of it is that he has had rather considerable doses of radiation himself, and Dr. Montelius concurs with me in thinking that it, together with the weightlessness, may have affected his mind. Not in a dangerous sense, you understand, but by confirming his obstinate determination to carry out his orders at all costs.

Duruy considered. It certainly did cut down on one's thinking powers; he himself had found it harder to make the necessary calculations than it was after his arrival. "But what can I do about it?" he said at last.

"I thought that a personal appeal from you, one not on an official basis, might carry more weight."

"I don't think it would," said Duruy, thinking that the reason for Keenan's intimacy was quite different than what the doctor imagined. The skipper had certainly been in a foul mood lately, he had to admit.

"Moreover," Halvorsson went on, "it's simply mad to press this construction project, now that the Russian station is so close to being destroyed by that asteroid. We'll have the only station there is, and the only possibility of delivering atomic bombs that will hit their targets."

"I think Keenan knows that."

"Please." The doctor laid a hand on his arm. "The only alternative is to call the rest of the crew together and demand some action that would result in the deposition of the captain. I am responsible for the lives of the men on this station."

Duruy looked at him sharply. If Halvorsson was the Russian agent, this might be the opening wedge to something else. He got up, saying, "Well, I'll try it, but I won't guarantee the results. The captain is perfectly capable of telling me to go to hell too."

As he turned to leave the cabin the annunciator bell clanged. "Mr. Duruy! Mr. Duruy!" the machine bawled. "Report at once to the observatory."

Duruy hurried out to where the corridor branched, one line going off at a steep angle upward, seized the guide rail and pulled himself into a position with his feet in the place where his right elbow had been, and hurried along the new "floor." The hatch leading to the bubble-like dome of the observatory was open overhead. He reached up and pulled himself lightly in, to find Keenan, MacCartney, and Etchardy staring out at the brilliant points of fire that made up the Milky Way.

The captain said, "You understand Portuguese, don't you?"

"The Brazilian version of it, I do. Why?"

"What does this say?" He shoved a piece of paper forward onto the lectern where a small light burned. Duruy felt the blood rush tumultuously to his face as he read:

Tem a estação Senhor Duruy

It was all he could do to find voice to say, "It's a question, and it asks whether Mr. Duruy is at the station."

Keenan's voice had an edge of coldness. "Tell him, Mac."

MacCartney indicated the telescope. "If you'll look through there you'll see the Russian station. That black duodecahedron that shuts out some of the stars. About a week ago when Etchardy was watching it, he noticed there were flashing lights on the exterior. He thought they might be signals and called me in. We kept watching and they were signals all right, in International Morse, using English, and directed to us. The Russians had discovered that they were about to be wiped out by an asteroid and wanted us to come take them off."

Keenan broke in. "I had Mac rig some big searchlights of our own, and told them to go chase themselves."

Duruy said, "Why?"

"Isn't it pretty obvious? If they really wanted to be taken off they could signal for their service ship—or one of them, they may have more. Not at all; they wanted to get us up there where we'd be involved in the smash. I figured out the time it would take to change orbit to match theirs, and it would be just about right. Or else they were going to get us in so close they could let us have it with a torpedo. Now comes this."

An unreasonable hope, accompanied by a black fear, began to surge in Duruy. He said, "Well, they know I'm out here, anyway. I don't suppose it would do any harm to answer and find out what they want."

MacCartney glanced at Keenan, who nodded. "What shall I send?" asked the communicator.

"Just *sim*."

MacCartney reached over and touched a key. The interior of the observatory was momentarily lit by a series of pulsating flashes as the message tapped out. Etchardy applied his eye to the telescope. "They got it all right. Here comes the answer."

MacCartney switched places with him and began reading off the letters as they came over. "I-n-f-o-r-m-a-l-o . . ."

Duruy copied the message down, and then read:

" 'Tell him that the girl he met at the Maricá wedding asks his help.' "

The others were looking at him queerly. "What does it mean?" said Keenan.

"I met a girl at a party in Brazil and—and got to like her a good deal. She turned out to be a Russian."

"And now they claim she's out there. I'm going to get to the bottom of this. Ask her to prove it's the same one," said Keenan.

"She mentioned the Maricá wedding, where we met," said Duruy.

"No proof. Anyone could have learned of that from her. Ask her for something that will show it's the same one." Keenan's voice was harsh.

Duruy frowned, concentrated, and put the idea into Portuguese. No one spoke; under the double glass dome it was chilly in the observatory in spite of the heaters busily transmitting warmth from the sunward side of Project Excelsior. MacCartney slowly read off the letters of the reply.

"What does it say?" demanded Keenan.

Duruy felt as though he were choking. "It says, 'Tell him she meant everything she said the last night in Brazil.' "

"All right, what does it mean?" demanded the captain inexorably.

"She said that she loved me." Duruy's hands gripped the lectern, and from the corner of his eye he could see Etchardy looking at him with something like pity.

"Then you're satisfied she's up there? Ask why they can't get help from their own service ship."

Once more there was the thick silence as the message flashed out and they waited for the reply. MacCartney didn't understand the structure of the Portuguese words, and the letters ran together.

Duruy translated. "It says that they didn't find out about the approach of the asteroid until three days ago, and their service ship can't be ready to take off for eleven days more, when it will be too late."

Keenan snorted. "And those bastards think they have the know-how to keep up with us! Etchardy had it spotted five weeks ago. All right, put this into your damned spiggoty language—if we approach, our station will be caught in the crash, too, and what good will that do anybody?"

Duruy said, "Captain."

"Well, what is it?"

"There's another way of helping them. As I understand it from Etchardy, the mass of that asteroid is not so enormous. With the improved atomic warheads, two or three of our torpedoes would blow it into dust. I'm sure I could calculate orbits to hit it."

"You are, are you? All right, then, send this message; send it in English, Mac. 'American station advises Russian station to use the torpedoes intended for American cities in protecting itself from asteroid.'"

Once more there was the flicker of light as the message was transmitted. Duruy wondered what part of the earth they were over now, and whether the observers at their telescopes down there were picking up this interchange of messages. There would be a commotion at White Sands, and even in the chaste corridors of the Pentagon.

"They're sending again," said MacCartney. "Here it comes, in English this time. 'We—have—expended—all—four—torpedoes—without—hitting—object.'"

"So they want us to use ours," said Keenan. "Ha! I wonder if they think anyone believes they had only four torpedoes. Typical Russki piece of business—the big lie. Tell them the answer is no."

Etchardy drew a deep breath. Duruy said, "Captain, it could be they only did have four. At the staff conference Colonel le Maistre developed the fact that their station was having a lot of trouble with weights. And they aren't so good with the calculator, either, we know that. They could have missed."

Keenan shook his head. "This station is part of the defense system of the Western Allies, and I cannot dissipate its resources as the result of a request from the Russians, who have always lied to us and failed to keep their engagements with us. This is nothing more or less than the old proposition to disarm both stations, which was rejected long ago on earth. The answer is still no."

Duruy put out a hand and cried desperately, "But she took a chance on her own life to save me! You can't do this. It's a matter——" He felt tears struggling at the corners of his eyes and gulped to hold them back.

Keenan merely looked at him. "Etchardy," he said, "take over the watch in calculation. Duruy, I want you to come with me."

He stepped to the hatch and leaped down, leading the way to his own cabin and locking the door. Then he faced Duruy.

"Lambert," he said, "I like you personally. I think you've done the right kind of work out here. But I wonder if you're aware of exactly what your position is."

"What do you mean?"

Keenan elevated a hand and began to tick points off on his fingers. "You were mixed up with this woman, this Soviet spy, in South America. You've just admitted that your relations with her were close. You tried to write her a letter after briefing and before coming aboard this station. You are trying to persuade me to take a step which is equivalent to the Russian proposition for disarming this station. Has it occurred to you that if we start looking for a Russian agent aboard the evidence fits you better than anyone else? Has it occurred to you that this might be one of the reasons for keeping you close to me all the time and not letting you be alone with other members of the crew?"

Duruy stared at him, for a moment without a word to say. What was the use of protesting? It was true, that was the evidence, only . . . Then a sudden flare of anger enveloped him as he thought of the conversation with Dr. Halvorsson.

"Look here," he said, "if you want to put a special explanation on what people do, you can make out a case against almost anyone. Even yourself—you've got half the crew down with radiation disease now, and by the time the relief ship can get here, we may all be dead."

Keenan ran a tongue around his lips. "That's my business as commander of this station. Go to your cabin and think over what I've said."

Duruy's feet dragged him to the door, and he sat down heavily in his own compartment. Montelius was right. Keenan was getting beyond reason. But that wouldn't be much help to Tina, out there in that steel duodecahedron. He supposed he would have to think of her as Tatiana, now, but that didn't make much difference, either. The menacing bulk of Albert was rushing toward her like a fate, there would be one brief, flaring crash out there under the stars, and then . . .

Damn the Russians, why were they so incompetent with their caclulator? It would be so easy to prevent. The orbit would have to be a spiral, of course; they'd probably missed out by calculating a direct-line approach to the asteroid.

He began to go over in his mind the steps he would take in feeding the problem to the machine. At that distance it would be simple; nowhere near as difficult as setting up the calculation for a problem that involved an approach through atmosphere.

Then his mind leaped back to the other problem of the Russian agent aboard—if there was one. If there was one, and he could find out who it was, even Keenan might be convinced. The trouble was that the triple problems of the agent, weightlessness, and the lack of the service ship were driving the captain half mad. If he could somehow be relieved of one of them . . . But who could it be? Not Long. Not Etchardy. Halvorsson? Montelius? One of the mechanics?

With his mind whirling round these problems, Duruy fell into a kind of uneasy doze in his chair.

IX

☐ Long wakened him to accompany him to the main cabin for the meal before going on watch. Still occupied with his problem, Duruy munched away almost mechanically, thinking of what Halvorsson had said—that the only alternative might be to call the crew together and depose the captain. That would solve Halvorsson's difficulty, and possibly his too. If it were done soon enough so that he could be allowed to fire the torpedoes at Albert.

But would any attempt to get rid of Keenan work? Long, MacCartney, the reserve communicator were officers, and most of the crew high-ranking petty officers, long bred in the habit of obedience to authority. Halvorsson was a civilian, so was he. It would take an extraordinarily convincing speaker to line up such servicemen against the captain, and Duruy didn't think he filled the role. Neither did Halvorsson, for that matter, with his brusque manner and insistence on being right. And if the crew were called together for such a purpose Keenan had a means of deadly counterattack. He would, as he had in the cabin last night, accuse Duruy of being a Russian agent, and present the evidence. The fact that Duruy was part of a movement to depose him would be all the more convincing in such a case.

And even if the captain were deposed, what then? What view would General Gebhard take of it? Mutiny. And the new commander, whoever he was, might be no more willing to expend torpedoes to save the Russian station. Still, Tina—Tatiana had risked her own life to save him; he must take the chance. . . .

As he thought of her Lambert Duruy suddenly realized what he was eating, and where he had eaten it before.

"This is not really a Brazilian recipe at all," she had said. *"I learned it in Paris from an old Hungarian woman there."* And Hungary was a Soviet country; and Tina had been a Soviet agent.

Long was staring at him from across the table. "Just wake up?" he said.

"Yes," said Duruy, "I think I did. Who cooked this mess, anyway?"

"Grandissi, of course. What's the matter with it? I think he's pretty hot with a skillet."

"Hotter than a rocket blast," said Duruy grimly. "In fact so hot that somebody's likely to get burned. Come with me for a minute. I want you to hear what's said."

The puzzled-looking Long followed him to the window which gave on the galley. "Grandissi!" called Duruy. "What do you call this stuff you served us?"

The small man looked up. "You liked it? It is called veal Zingara."

"I see. Is it an Italian dish? Where did you learn to cook it?"

"No, it is not Italian. It is—is—I don't remember. I think I got it from a cookbook sometime. Don't remember." His face suddenly went sullen and he turned his back.

Duruy pulled Long out into the corridor. "Come on to the skipper's cabin. This is important."

"What's it all about?"

"Tell you when we get there. He'll be just getting ready to go on watch."

Keenan looked ill as he opened the door. The strain was telling on him badly, Duruy realized, with a sudden rush of sympathy. He said, "Captain, I think I have identified your Russian agent."

"Russian agent?" said Long, looking from one to the other, and the captain: "Whom do you accuse?"

"Grandissi, the torpedo machinist."

"What grounds have you for accusing him?"

"When I knew this girl, the one who is now in the Russian station, she cooked a dinner for me one night. It was a dish called veal Zingara, which she said she had learned from a Hungarian woman. Grandissi has just served us with veal Zingara."

Keenan threw back his head and gave a hard laugh. "And you expect me to call him up on the strength of that?"

"No. It only gives us a lead for where to look. In addition, just before the take-off, I heard him quoting Marxian doctrine to one of the mechanics."

"Lots of people can quote Marx. In fact I can do it myself."

Duruy said, "I realize this isn't conclusive. As Colonel le Maistre once said, nothing ever is when you're dealing with spies. But don't you remember, when we were talking about this on the first day aboard, we were trying to figure out what an agent here could possibly accomplish? Well, think. There's just one man on the station, aside from the calculator, who could make the torpedoes useless. That's the torpedo machinist. He could change the controls, the feed, the wing angle, any one of half a dozen things, so they wouldn't fly true."

"That's true," said Keenan, rubbing his chin, "but——"

"May I suggest how we can find out? Let's have one of the mechanics we're sure of—say Beckwith or Jablotsky—check the adjustments on some of the older torpedoes that Grandissi hasn't worked on against some of those he has. Say Number Two against Number Twenty-nine, or Four against Thirty. A random choice. No, a couple of them. He may have been after some of the older ones too. Then if we find anything wrong we can call him in and question him, or have Dr. Montelius try hypnotism or a shot of scopolamine."

Keenan's brows knitted. Then he lifted his head. "You're right. I can't afford to take the chance of not investigating this to the hilt. Long, you're coming off watch and I'm just going on. Get Beckwith and have him make an examination of those torpedoes under your personal supervision. If you find anything wrong, seal up Grandissi's machine shop, grab him quick, and hold him in main cabin. Better go armed." He flashed a glance at Duruy. "But what I said before still goes. I'm taking you up to Calculation now."

Inside the calculation room Etchardy greeted Duruy with a silent handclasp that bespoke sympathy and belief, but neither of them said anything. The order sheet said that Number Thirty-four should be calculated to fall on Sverdlovsk, but after a few minutes with the problem Duruy shoved it aside and began to work out the spiral orbit that would carry the torpedo to Albert. What the hell! If the station and its inhabitants survived that long he'd have an extra three months to do all the calculating necessary for earth landings, and if there were any perturbations in Project Excelsior's movement there would have to be some recalculation anyway.

The spiral-orbit problem was a nasty one; the machine twice rejected the data he fed it as leading to "No solution," and he became so absorbed in the task that he did not notice the passage of time until the annunciator bell clanged and the machine said, "Mr. Duruy. To the main cabin."

The place was crowded when he arrived, Keenan seated behind the table at the end of the room, while before him stood Long and Beckwith, gripping Grandissi by the arms.

"Are all the officers and civilians here now?" said the captain, glancing around.

"All but MacCartney. He's on watch, covering the Russian station," said someone, and Keenan leaned forward.

"I constitute this a court of trial," he said formally. "Dr. Montelius, will you record the proceedings? Now, Beckwith, tell us what you found."

Almost as though he were reciting, the mechanic said, "According to orders and under the direction of Captain Long, I inspected torpedo Number Seven and torpedo Number Twenty-five. I found that the main connecting-rod wing attachments in Twenty-five were cut nearly through and the cut filled with magnalium alloy. Upon further inspection I found this was true also in Numbers Twenty-seven, Twenty-eight, and Twenty-nine."

"Did you examine any others?"

"No, sir. Captain Long said this was sufficient."

"What would the effect be if the torpedo was fired?"

Beckwith hesitated a minute. "It would behave all right at the start, I think, sir. But if the torpedo struck air or anything like that, I think the wings would rip off."

Keenan said, "Mr. Duruy, what would happen if a torpedo's wings ripped off on entering the atmosphere?"

Duruy said, "I haven't the least idea. The heat generated by its passage through the air might turn it into a meteor. Or it might set off the trigger mechanism and give it a high air burst. Or it might be carried deep underground and explode there. It certainly wouldn't strike anywhere near the place it was calculated for."

"In other words, those torpedoes were thoroughly sabotaged. Beckwith, how long would it take to make them good?"

"Gee, Captain, I don't know. I ain't no torpedo machinist, I'm just a mechanic. But I don't think we got any more stock like those main connecting-rod wing attachments aboard, and if we have to machine them, it would take a hell of a time."

Keenan said, "Grandissi, you were in charge of the assembly of those torpedoes. What have you got to say about how they got damaged?"

The man's face was sullen. "Nothing."

"Who else could have done it?"

Grandissi did not answer.

Keenan looked around. "Does any member of this court believe that anyone but Grandissi could have been guilty?"

The man's composure suddenly broke. "I demand my rights!" he screamed, twisting in the grip of his captors. "This is a kangaroo court! I have a right to a fair trial. You haven't any evidence against me!"

"You have no rights," said Keenan sternly. "I am the captain of this station, and the regulations say my authority is absolute in cases of sabotage or attempted sabotage. I don't even need to call this court, except to inform them of what's going on. Now do you want to talk?"

"Not to a kangaroo court."

"We'll see about that. Dr. Montelius, will you administer a little scopolamine to this man?"

The doctor picked up a small black case and worked toward Grandissi among the tables. The man's head turned and his eyes rolled up till the whites were almost visible; then something else snapped in him, and he yelled, "All right, you imperialist rats, I did it! I did it, and I'm glad of it! A lot of good it will do you to know it—you'll all be dead of the two-fifties before you can do anything about it!"

There was a stir and murmur in the narrow cabin. Keenan said, "There's one thing we can do about it, and right away. I condemn you to be ejected from Number Three airlock——"

A series of relays suddenly clicked home in Duruy's brain, and he remembered Colonel le Maistre tweaking his long mustache and Dr. Mahovitzov's pleased expression over the statement that the Western Allies had no cure for the two-fifties. He called out:

"Pardon me, Captain, but may I ask this man a question?"

Keenan's voice was noticeably more friendly than it had been before. "If you think you can get anything useful out of him."

"Just one question, and it will be very much to his interest to answer. Grandissi, do the Russians have a cure for the two-fifties?"

"None of your damned business, imperialist filth."

Duruy threw up his hands. "You're writing your own sentence, Grandissi," he said, and turned to Keenan again. "I think they do. In fact I'm almost sure they do, and so is Colonel le Maistre. Look, Captain, we have those torpedoes that won't hit anything on earth, but out here in space where there's no air pressure, they're perfectly good. The wings don't even matter. I can vector them in on Albert and save the Russian station. I suggest we signal them and offer to do it if they will cure our cases of the two-fifties for us."

Keenan's face became hard again. "I have already answered that question. No."

Dr. Halvorsson spoke up. "Captain, this station will be entirely inoperative in another three months, as a result of radiation disease. I think that anything which promises to save us from it is justified."

Montelius nodded his head. "So do I."

Keenan said, "Long, what's your opinion on this?"

"I think they're right, sir. You can look at it like this: there isn't much use going on with the construction program when the torpedoes for it are disabled. And even if our lives don't matter, the replacement crew that came out here when they got the *Goddard* repaired or a new one built would find a stock of torpedoes that didn't work right, and they wouldn't even know they were sour. But if they can fix up the two-fifties for us we can wait as long as necessary for relief."

Keenan said, "How do we know they can do it? I wouldn't believe this animal"—he gestured toward Grandissi—"even if he had the Bible to prove what he said, and the rest of them can tell lies just as fast. Etchardy, do you agree with the others?"

The navigator nodded. "What can they take from us if we make one contact? It's not a general pacification, but a treaty between us and the Russian station to save both. And I think there is good reason to believe that they have at least a prevention of the two-fifties, and if that, probably a cure also. Dr. Halvorsson, who of all this crew shows the least effect of radiation?"

The doctor thought a moment, then started. "Grandissi!"

"Exactly," said Etchardy. "And he has been working at the torpedo tubes, which are outside the air and water storage area. Oh, he has been working at them hard, to make all those cuts in the wings. Before the take-off they must have given him an injection or something to prevent. Isn't that true, Grandissi?"

The man's face had gone sullen again. "I say nothing," he said.

"You don't have to." Keenan looked around the room. "The vote seems to be unanimous. I don't agree, but I'll concede the point. Long and Beckwith, take care of that man. Duruy, will you set up the necessary calculations, while I go up to the observatory and see if I can get into communication with those people?"

X

☐ Duruy sat at the calculating table, with the intercom headset clamped over his ears. There was the gentlest of pressures at the small of his back as Project Excelsior swung slowly through the arc that would bring her torpedo tubes to bear on Albert.

The data sheets were before him. From up in the dome of the observatory Etchardy's voice carried a string of figures to his ears: "Azimuth two-zero-point-one-six; line zero-zero-point-seven-one; elevation no change; azimuth two-one-point-zero-two . . ."

His fingers played over the keys. The skin felt tight across his face and his head ached with the effect of twelve uninterrupted hours of concentrated labor at the big board. He spoke into the mike:

"Observatory, stand by to report trail of torpedo. Your points are Zeta Pisces, Beta Pegasus . . . Torpedo room, stand by; thirty seconds—twenty-five—twenty —fifteen—ten seconds—five—four—three—two—one— fire Twenty-seven!"

The whole station rocked to the shock of the discharge. Etchardy's voice came down the wire: "Running two seconds low, running two seconds low," and Duruy punched two keys, read off the result, then tripped the control that would send an automatic radio signal to the speeding torpedo, directing it to fire a three-second blast from the lower ejection tube and lift its nose into the proper spiral for the target.

"On course, on course," reported Etchardy.

Keenan's voice cut into the circuit. "Ready with Twenty-eight."

Duruy glanced at his data sheets. "No, Captain, don't dare risk that one without a new approach. The only good course will carry it too close to the Russian station. Take Twenty-five or Twenty-nine."

There was an inarticulate gurk on the line, then after a moment's wait: "Ready with Twenty-nine."

"Observatory, report bearings."

Etchardy's voice began droning again: "Azimuth two-two-point-three-nine, line . . ."

"Fire Twenty-nine!"

Once more the station quivered in response to the discharge and a mechanical pencil leaped from the console where Duruy had placed it, drifting toward the deck with the deliberation of a scrap of paper. He glanced over the data sheets again and, as Keenan's voice assured him that the torpedo destined for the town of Uralskoi was ready for firing, set himself to work out the effect of the minor changes in the station's position caused by the firing of the two torpedoes.

"Fire Twenty-five!"

This one developed a yaw and had to be corrected heavily. Duruy applied the necessary factors, leaned back, and said, "I think that's all we can do now, Captain. Permission to visit observatory and see results."

"Permission granted."

Keenan himself and MacCartney were already under the dome when Duruy arrived. "How are they running?" he asked.

The atmosphere was notably different than the last time the four had been there together. "Lost them," said Etchardy. "All three have stopped firing. But I'm watching Albert for results. Duruy, if you get direct hits I'll swear you're the greatest calculator in history. Albert's only three miles in diameter."

"I haven't too much confidence in Twenty-nine," said Duruy. "That was a very tricky orbit. But if we get one hit out of the first two, a grazer will do for the third one. It will arrive while the atomic explosion's still going on, and that ought to trigger it, hadn't it, Captain?"

"Yes," said Keenan, and then checked. He turned to Etchardy. "Where are we with relation to the earth?"

"Just about over the Sahara. We won't pass White Sands again until the next revolution."

The captain said, "Mac, does that code book of yours provide any way of saying that the action we have taken is unavoidable? There'll be some telescopes in North Africa where they're sure to pick up the fact that we've fired torpedoes and report it."

MacCartney said, "I'll try." He laughed. "I just wonder what the Russians down there are thinking about now after seeing us let loose those torpedoes. I don't think they're going to like the idea very well."

"They ought to know we couldn't hit any of their cities from this angle," said Duruy, "even with a spiral. Anyway, they'll find out soon enough."

"What worries me more is what they'll say about this at White Sands. If they put out a message disapproving, I'm going to resign my commission." He sighed, and in the dim light of the observatory they could see his face was haggard.

MacCartney began, "Captain——"

"Sssh," said Duruy, watching the clock. "We ought to know in less than a minute now."

Etchardy snapped the sun shield into position over the telescope's eyepiece and gazed into it intently. The others followed the pointing finger of the tube. Suddenly the navigator gave a little cry; the three men in the observatory with him saw a little point of light, redder than Mars when viewed from the earth, that grew and spread and turned to the white heat of the center of a furnace of intolerable brilliance till it seemed to fill a whole sector of the heavens, then as abruptly diminished.

MacCartney slapped Duruy on the back. "You did it!" he shouted.

"With Number Twenty-seven, anyway," said Duruy. "I hope that will be enough by itself. It ought to knock whatever is left of Albert out of his course, but I don't know."

"The Russian station is showing lights," said Etchardy. "Want to take over and read their message?"

"Okay," said MacCartney. "Here it is: 'Russian—station — thanks — you — hopes — more — than — one — torpedo — sent — as — object — still — approaches.'"

Keenan said, "Duruy, is there time to fire another shot if the other two miss?"

"Just about," said Duruy, "counting the time necessary to swing our station. But not all the new tubes may bear right."

"I can't sanction any use of the first twenty-four," said Keenan. "They haven't been sabotaged and are still useful against earthly targets."

Duruy looked at the clock. "We may have to. I think Twenty-nine's going to be a miss."

"I still can't sanction the first twenty-four," persisted the captain.

"Let's hope Twenty-five does it, then," said Duruy, and all four were silent, watching the heavens. There was a loud clicking from the power-driven clock. Duruy could not seem to keep his eyes away from it, though the second hand seemed barely to crawl across its surface. Keenan drew a deep breath; Etchardy was watching with fascinated attention. "Now——" began Duruy, but even as he spoke the great flare burst out again, wider and redder than before.

"Albert's gone!" cried Etchardy as the flame died. "There isn't enough of him to pick up in the telescope."

Keenan turned to the three. "I think they'll probably have a slightly radioactive meteor shower in the Sahara in a couple of days," he said. "All right, Mac, put a general announcement of this on the annunciator system. Duruy, do you want to come up to Control with me and work out the orbit change for contacting the Russian station?"

XI

☐ From outside a series of metallic bumps and scrapings rang through Project Excelsior as the two stations pursued their way through space, barely in physical contact. Inside, Captain Keenan held up a hand and promptly bumped against one of the tables of the main cabin, which were hanging from the ceiling, now that the angle of their approach and the Russian's greater mass had given the American station just enough gravity in that direction to turn the old ceiling into a floor.

"Now I want you all to understand," said the captain, "that this is nothing but a truce between the two stations. The Russians have kept their part of the agreement loyally thus far, but I'm convinced that it's because we have enough torpedoes to blow them all to bits. I think they'll keep their agreement not to let their service ship come up until we have resumed a normal orbit, but only for the same reason. They're still as suspicious as ever and not taking any chances. They haven't allowed any of our crew aboard their station and the doctor they have sent over won't even allow Dr. Halvorsson or Dr. Montelius to be present when he administers the injections. However, as you all know, the injections have definitely worked. All our cases have recovered during the past two weeks, and they show no signs of relapse. Am I not correct, Doctor? Good; now I want to say that the conduct of this crew has been very good during the period of contact with the Russian station, and I want it to remain that way. The temporary regulations made at the time of contact are still in force, even though we're going to cast off and start rockets tomorrow, and some of you might like to make a little contact or obtain a souvenir. No one to use suits for any purpose except Captain Long and the two men who meet the Russian doctor in the air lock. All corridors except that leading from the air lock to this cabin to remain closed while he is aboard. No signaling. That's all. All right, Duruy, you wanted to see me?"

He led the way along the corridor to his own cabin and squatted on the floor, since the furniture, like that in the main compartment, was now attached to the ceiling. "I'll be damned glad when we do break free," he said. "I'm getting rather tired of cold food, even if they have managed to supply us with hot coffee from that hot plate Grey rigged. What is it, Lambert?"

Duruy said, "I want an exception to those temporary regulations, Captain."

Keenan frowned. "What kind?"

"I want to get in touch with—Miss Vsevolod."

"It can't be done. Are you insane? Not only did you consort with this Russian agent on earth, but now you want to meet her out here in space, where both of us are doing all we can to keep whatever secrets we have."

"I rather thought you'd feel that way about it. But may I point out that if I hadn't been in—touch with her the Russians in that station would all be dead by now, and most of your crew would be facing hopeless cases of the two-fifties."

The intercom rang. "Keenan," said the captain.

"This is Etchardy. The fragments of Albert are spreading out very near our old orbit. I am pretty well satisfied they're going to form a ring around the earth, like the ones around Saturn."

"Is it important?"

"No, only decorative—unless one of the service ships runs into it."

"I'll take it up later. Busy now." Keenan cut the intercom and faced Duruy again. "I'm aware that both stations have benefited by the contact. But that doesn't make a repetition of it desirable or anything less than dangerous. They certainly wouldn't allow you aboard their station, and I'm certainly not going to allow a Russian, and a rocket technician at that, in Project Excelsior. What do you expect to do? Stand out there in space and hold hands through your suits?"

"Captain," said Duruy, "have you ever been in love?" He felt his hands perspiring violently, and remembered the interview with General Gebhard.

"Several times," said Keenan promptly. "But it doesn't make any difference. You'll just have to keep your emotional involvements down on earth, where they belong. This is space."

"But can't I send her a message?"

"When we're back in our orbit, by means of the lights, maybe. Not now. I'll consider it——"

The intercom called his attention again. "Keenan," he said.

"This is Long. Russian doctor coming aboard to give Mr. Duruy his preventive shot."

"Very well." The captain stood up. "Come along. You're the last one on the list and as soon as this is over we can cast loose and get some decent food. As I said before, when we're back in our normal orbit I'll consider a message through lights. You can date her up for a meeting on earth, if you want to take the chance. But not now. Since we've been following the Russian orbit we haven't received any messages from White Sands and the last ones we got weren't encouraging."

He had been moving along the corridor toward the main cabin as he talked. As he opened the door the intercom sounded again. "Is Captain Keenan in the main cabin?" came Long's voice.

"Speaking."

"Russian doctor is a woman."

Duruy's heart began to beat wildly. Keenan turned and gave him a long, stern look. "Very well," he said into the machine. "Bring her along. I'm here."

He looked at Duruy again. "If that is——" he began, but didn't finish the sentence.

Duruy arranged himself against the bulkhead. There were steps outside, the door opened, and through it, preceded by Long, came Tina Castelhoso.

She gave a little cry and launched herself across the room into Duruy's arms. Long blew his nose, the men with him closed the door behind them. Even Keenan's voice was a little shaky as he said:

"Madam, didn't you come here to give Mr. Duruy a treatment?"

She turned out of the circle of Duruy's arms and shook her head. "No. I am coming here for to stay. For always."

"I don't believe that my orders permit——"

The insistent intercom called again. "Captain Keenan, this is MacCartney. Russian station is signaling."

"Very well. Repeat the message to me here. I cannot leave at present."

MacCartney's voice came metallically from the device. "Message. 'Russian — station — demands — return — of Soviet — citizen — Vsevolod — wanted — for — trial — on — treason — charges.'"

Keenan took one look at the pair, now again fiercely clutched in each other's arms. Duruy said, "Tell him you claim the right of asylum."

"I claim asylum," said Tina obediently.

Keenan gave a lopsided grin. "All right, you win. MacCartney!"

"Yes, sir."

"Send as follows: 'Demand refused. Person in question is now acquiring American citizenship by marriage.'" He turned toward the pair. "I am the captain of a ship at a distance from land, and I believe that I am permitted to perform the ceremony."

THE WANDERER'S RETURN

I

☐ "Signal from the flagship, sir," said little Benton, and handed up one of the familiar blue forms.

Commodore Alstair Lortud swung round on the platform in the observation bubble and glanced over his shoulder. Even out here at a hundred miles above the planet's surface streamers of smoke were still shooting past, propelled by the boiling tumult of incandescent gases below. "I don't know what there is left to signal about," he said. "That place won't even be fit for algal life for another hundred years." He shuddered slightly.

"They had it coming. In fact they started——" began Captain Pelham, and stopped as Lortud unfolded the form and held up a hand.

"Listen to this," he said. " 'Admiral MacKinnon to Commodore Lortud: Well done, Earth contingent. Operation against Ilya now completed. You are released from control of United Planets command as of 1123: 28XZ galactic time.' Nothing more to do but go home and pin on the medals, I guess, Captain."

A tall blond officer with the stripes of a commander gazed at the burning tumult below. "Somebody else can have mine for this job," he said. "I'm not particularly proud of burning up a whole world and everyone on it."

Captain Pelham gave a short bark of a laugh. "They

Copyright, 1951, by Standard Magazines, Inc. Originally published in December, 1951, *Thrilling Wonder Stories*.

really ought to condition you psychological officers along with the rest of us—at least when you're going on punitive service," he said, and turned to the commodore.

"Shall I notify the squadron?"

"I'll send it. Benton! Take the following: 'Commodore Lortud to all ships, Earth Squadron: Operation completed. We are released from United Planets command. Squadron will proceed to point on present bearing, azimuth 22' " —he glanced at the repeater instrument board—" 'arc 261. Orbit around *Massachusetts* there while reporting any deficiencies and casualties beyond those already indicated before setting course for home.' . . . Wait a minute, Benton. Add this—'Admiral MacKinnon sends us his well done. Commodore Lortud adds his heartiest appreciation to all hands, especially to *Bayern* for her gallant conduct in late battle.' " He swung toward the psychological officer. "That last okay with you, Yurka?"

The commander nodded. "Very much all right. Those Germans need to be told they're not only as good as anyone else but a little bit better. And the *Bayern* certainly did take us off the hook when that Ilyan tried to ram."

Captain Pelham picked up the intercom phone and gave the orders that would carry the *Massachusetts* out to the rendezvous point named by the commodore, then turned back to the other two.

"I still can't quite understand it," he said. "You'd think that even if they were beaten in a war and had to surrender they'd want to stay alive and try to build something. They must have known that they couldn't hope to discourage the whole United Planets force, even after they made those suicide crashes into the *Corrientes* and those six ships from 221 Aurigae. But they kept right on trying."

The ship tilted and the view from the bubble changed from the smoking ruin of a planet to the outer stars of Corona Borealis. Yurka said, "It's perfectly explainable if you know something about the history of psychology.

The Ilyans were infected with something the old psychologists used to call *Schadenfreude*, which means, roughly, taking pleasure in destruction."

"It's still hard to understand," said the captain. "A disease?"

"A psychological one. It was supposed to have been bred out of the whole human race a couple of thousand years ago, but it was fairly common way back when Earth was the only inhabited planet. One of the main reasons why they used to have wars. The fact that you people are moderns and haven't a trace of it is the reason why they had to give you all that psych conditioning before sending you out on this junket."

Commodore Lortud said, "But look here. If they can condition us to be willing to destroy the Ilyans, why couldn't they condition the Ilyans in the other direction?"

Yurka grinned. "You know the old recipe for rabbit stew? First catch your rabbit. That is, they wouldn't let themselves be taken for the purpose. And you saw how those few prisoners we had behaved. The minute we got to working on them they told us just where the atombomb stockpiles were located and what the intentions of the Ilyan command were. They were so rotten with *Schadenfreude* that they were willing to see their own people destroyed, just as long as something went up. Only——"

"Only what?" said Pelham.

"Only I can't help thinking that it's too bad we had to do for the whole planet. There must have been some brilliant minds down there."

"Too damned brilliant," growled Pelham. "When they set up that field that lowered all the electrical potentials and grabbed those three ships from Gamma Ceti, I thought we were in for real trouble. And they might have gone on from there if the Council hadn't sent us here before they were really ready to make a big plunge at something."

"I suppose you're right." Yurka sighed. "From my point of view, though, it's still too bad that we coouldn't have studied enough of them for long enough to determine how this infection became so widespread. What kind of a colony was it?"

"I can tell you that," observed Commodore Lortud, "because, as it happens, I've just been looking over some of the old family papers from the days when the first Lortud discovered the neptunium mines on E Centauri. Ilya was a mixed colony, settled by soldiers from eastern Europe in one of the old wars. They made it a closed planet as soon as the regulations allowed. Wouldn't accept commercial space traffic even. That's why it was so hard to catch up with them when they started raiding ships and raising hell generally. The Council thought it was accidental at first, and didn't know that they had a gang full of this—what do you call it?—on their hands."

The repeater clanged to call attention and the trio in the observation bubble saw the speed indicator slip down to zero. The intercom buzzed. "Calling Captain Pelham," it said.

"Pelham here."

"Navigation. We have reached assigned position, in slow orbit around Ilya."

"Very well." The captain looked at Lortud, who said, "I suppose we'd better go up to Communications and get the reports. You can have them send on visual as soon as they get close enough."

He led the way, ducking his black, curly head through the door into the passage. A pair of cadets and a lieutenant saluted smartly and climbed into the observation bubble vacated by the senior officers. One of them said, "If I had that guy's money, nothing on Earth would make me come out here, a year and a half from home."

"If you had Lortud's money, everything off Earth would make you come," said the other. "The corporations are after the family holdings, but they can't do anything about it as long as he's in the service and turns up a job of exploration now and then."

Communications, like everything else aboard the big fighting ship, was squeezed into the smallest possible space, with just room for three seats before the two-foot screen used for visual communication. Lortud took one, Pelham the second; Major Purdy, the communicator, slipped around from the side of the screen and settled himself in the third, throwing the dimmer so that only an occasional flare from the spark-gaps above and beyond the screen lit the compartment. He cut in the switch, joggled a control once or twice, and the huge circular bulk of the *Invincible* filled the view plate, looking rather like a moon whose craters had been made regular and systematic. But the edge of one crater had the appearance of melted taffy.

"Come in, *Invincible*," said Purdy, and threw the switch for the communications beam. The vivid blue light played on Lortud's face; on the screen the picture of the space ship faded into that of her commander, one of the long-jawed British type that centuries had failed to alter.

"*Invincible*," he said. "We have six killed, three wounded, as a result of a hit near Tube Fourteen, which you doubtless noted. Ammunition remaining, 78 per cent. Fuel, 82 per cent. No significant air loss. We lost a water tank in the fighting day before yesterday, though, and we're a bit low. I'd appreciate being allowed to draw some before going into superspeed for the trip home. Also we have a 30 per cent deficiency in protein food."

The commodore turned to Captain Pelham. "Can we supply him?"

The captain picked up the intercom phone and spoke briefly to Supply, then said, "Sorry. We can't spare over a thousand pounds of proteins, and have only water enough ourselves for thirteen months of operation."

"And it will take us twelve to get back to the solar

system," murmured Lortud. "No factor of safety. How the hell did that happen? All right, *Invincible*. We will have you draw from one of the other ships. Resume orbit, and thank you."

The communicating light snapped off, the picture of the retreating *Invincible* came on the screen and walked across it to the edge as she circled the flagship, while the *Gloire* moved in to take her place. She had a smashed observation bubble, and a couple of men in suits were working on it, the flames of their torches glowing with electric brilliance on the side of the sphere that was turned away from the sun of doomed Ilya. She also reported a deficiency in protein foods and barely enough water for the homeward voyage.

Commodore Lortud frowned and made a note. The *Louisiana*, next to report, could spare some water, but not much. The *Miyako* had no water to spare and was short on proteins; the *Impero* was likewise short on water and the *Aquidaban* on protein foods. As the reports piled up Lortud became shorter and shorter, and when the last one was in he snapped:

"Purdy, get out an emergency signal to Admiral Mac-Kinnon at once. Tell him we urgently need a supply ship before departure for base. Pelham, call Hassinger and bring him up to my cabin. I want to find out why this expedition started out without enough supplies to get home on."

He stamped out of the compartment. Purdy switched on the lights and paused over the dials for fleet communication. "Pretty browned off, wasn't he? I'll bet somebody's head is going to roll."

"I don't know." Captain Pelham caressed the end of a white mustache. "When he's annoyed he just gets ingenious. The real time to worry is when he gets smooth and polite. The Lortuds are all like that. I knew his father."

"Odd name, though. What nationality is it?"

"American, like all of us for the past two thousand

years, or he'd be on one of the other ships. I think, though, that the family was Greek, back in the days of immigration. Well, I may as well get on with it."

He swung his way along the passage to the commodore's cabin at the center of the ship, where the nearness of the artificial gravity machine made it a job merely to stand up. A yeoman came out as he reached the door; Lortud was seated at his desk, going over the papers the man had brought with quick, strong fingers that betrayed no sign of the extra gravitational burden in the place. He motioned Pelham to a chair and did not look up until there was a knock at the door, and in answer to his "Come!" a lieutenant with the scroll of the supply service above his bars stepped in.

"Sit down, Hassinger," said the commodore. "Now there seems to be a little difficulty about the supply situation in the squadron, and I thought maybe you could help us clear it up." He smiled pleasantly.

"Yes, sir," said Hassinger.

"I notice from your report"—Lortud tapped it with his finger—"that you considered this ship adequately supplied for the expedition."

"Yes, sir."

"We've been out only a little over twenty months, and you were informed that this would probably be a very severe campaign, weren't you?"

"Yes, sir."

Lortud's fist came down on the desk. "Then how in the blistering hell does it come that we have barely enough supplies to get home on? How does it come that we haven't a gallon of water to give damaged ships of the squadron that need it? What would have happened if this campaign had lasted three months longer. Answer me, you congenital idiot, or I'll disrate you and set you to polishing dishes."

The lieutenant's thin face flushed. "Well, sir——"

"Answer me!"

Pelham cleared his throat in an effort to relieve the tension. "Sir," said Hassinger desperately, "I met the full squadron per capita requirements as laid down by the chief supply officer. We were informed that in view of the fact we would probably have heavy fighting we ought to go long on ammunition, because we could draw food and water from squadrons that didn't have to come such a distance as ours, and it would be fresher."

"As though we couldn't draw ammunition! Who was the illegitimate moron that thought up a doctrine like that?" He grabbed the papers and read: "De Santis."

There was a momentary silence. Pelham said, "Went out with the *Corrientes* when she was hit."

Hassinger said, "There's another thing, sir. After we got into action Commander Yurka required the issue of extra high-protein foods on psychological grounds. Our consumption has been abnormal."

"Damned witch doctor," growled Lortud.

Pelham said, "Part of this is either just bad luck or a matter of design, whichever way you want to put it, Commodore. The *Invincible* would have been all right for water if one of her tanks hadn't been hit, and it was pretty much the same with the *Dent Ardent*'s protein supply that the Ilyans pushed that small bacterial missile through on. I think we ought to report in favor of placing those essential life-sustaining supplies farther inboard and behind armor."

"Do that, will you, Pelham? For that matter . . ." he considered. "Perhaps we need a new cruiser class for very distant operation. If we're going to have to deal with any more gangs like the Ilyans, at the ends of the galaxy. The thing that makes me boil, though, is being forced to appeal for supplies to these damned colonials. Makes it look as though we were losing our grip back on the old mother planet. Next thing you know the Council will be declaring us a backward race and wanting to colnize *us*."

The intercom buzzed. Lortud picked it up, and the

other two saw his dark brows draw together again. He said, "Acknowledge. Try to contact any other squadron commander within range. I don't think you can do it, but try."

He laid the instrument down and turned. "Do you know who that was? Purdy. He says MacKinnon's in superspeed and can't be reached. That probably means that we'll have to land on a planet somewhere and pick up supplies. Must have been in an awful damned hurry to get out of here. Lieutenant Hassinger, inasmuch as you claim to have supplied the ship in accordance with a doctrine laid down by the squadron supply officer, and he's in a place where he can't confirm or deny it"—there was a grim smile around the commodore's lips—"you are not held responsible for the deficiencies of the original supply. However, you are held responsible for not protesting to me if this supply was inadequate according to your judgment, and for not reporting potential shortages before they became apparent. These items will appear in your record."

He stood up and the others imitated him. "Pelham, let's go down to Navigation and pick out a place where we can get some food and water. If there is any."

II

☐ Commander Eschelman, the navigator of the *Massachusetts*, spun his dividers across the star map.

"On distance from here, it's about a choice," he said. "We're almost midway between them. It's merely a matter of which one offers the better chance of getting what we want."

"They're both semiclosed," observed Pelham, looking thoughtfully at the catalogue of inhabited planets, "but that needn't affect us in this case. If we need food and water, to get some we certainly come under the head of distress landings."

"However, this Kushan place is nearer the Earth," said Lortud. "If we get what we want there we can shave about a week off the home trip. What do you think, Captain?"

Pelham said; "I don't know. If we miss out at Kushan it will take another six weeks to Asmara, then three more to get back to our original position, so we might not gain anything in the long run. And I'm not too happy about Kushan. It's marked here as an Indian colony, which means there's a good chance they're vegetarians, living on a low-protein diet. And proteins are specifically what we need."

"Dammit!" said Lortud. "I wish they'd listened to me when I wanted to bring a supply ship. We could convert."

"Read the dope on the stars again, will you, Holmgren?" said Pelham to the assistant navigator.

The young officer flipped over the pages. "Asmara is the third planet in the system of H.D. 100211," he read. "Region of Arcturus. Kushan is the second planet of H.D. 99571, region of Alpha Herculis, which is Ras Algethi. It's an F-5 type star."

"And the other's a G," said Pelham. "As long as you ask my opinion, Commodore, I think that settles it. Kushan will be a lot hotter planet, and as an Indian colony, they'll probably be living largely on fruits, juicy vegetables, and pulses. Besides, look here: Asmara's an Ethiopian colony, eighteen hundred years old. Weren't they a pastoral race back on Earth?"

"Ask Yurka," said Lortud. "He keeps track of those things. All right, Asmara it is, then. Plot a course, will you, Eschelman." He picked up the intercom and punched the button. "Communications? Take a general signal: 'Commodore Lortud to all ships: Have navigators plot course to H.D. 100211, Asmara. Report to Commander Eschelman for master computation not later than 1424: 28 ZX galactic time. Rig all ships for superspeed. As soon as computations are ready, cease orbiting and follow the flag.' Repeat that back to me."

The intercom gurked. "Very well," said Lortud, and turned to the others. "Gentlemen, I'm going to get a little sleep before the heat goes on. See you back at Australian space port."

He strode out, slightly swaggering. Eschelman looked after him and remarked, "Wonder which ship will make it first? Captain, I'll bet you a fiver that the *Dent Ardent* beats the gang."

Pelham shook his head. "You don't get me on that one. I know that fellow Hondschoote over there, and he's pretty good. If he were an American instead of a Dutchman, I'd have him up there in the chair where you are. What were you looking so hard at the commodore for?"

Eschelman said, "Feed the figures into the computer, will you, Holmgren? Why, Captain, I was just thinking that the boss displayed a startling interest in getting home for a man who was supposed to be conditioned for this expedition."

"I don't know." Pelham stroked his mustache. "Maybe the conditioning slipped after he got the release from the admiral. You'd have to ask Yurka about that. But God knows, he's got reason enough to hurry home."

"Why? To clip his coupons?"

"Did you ever meet Penny Lortud? She's one of the most beautiful women God ever made."

"Oh—oh," said Eschelman. "I thought the conditioning was supposed to keep our emotional lives straight, too, during the cruise."

"So it is. I was suggesting that in addition to the business involvement it might have some influence that he misses her."

From the side of the compartment Holmgren said; "Beg pardon, Commander. I have a tentative course calculated. Will you check it and take a fix?"

Pelham watched as the navigator ran quick, experienced fingers along the tape that had come from the calculating machine, then turned to the quartermaster. "Ready with the chronometer?" he said. "I'm going to fix on Xi Booti; Arcturus is too big at this distance, and won't give a true bearing." He applied his eye to the telescope, raised a hand, and called, "Mark!" then repeated the process for two more stars.

As he turned back to Pelham the latter said, "You fellows have it easy these days. When I was a navigator on the old *Reliance* we didn't have any such thing as the Lortud calculator; had to work out all the steps for ourselves."

"It was the commodore's father invented that, wasn't it?" said Eschelman. "By the way, you said something about his business involvements. I didn't know he had any except counting the money that rolled in."

"It's not as easy as that. The corporations, especially the Anthony Corp., have been trying to get their hooks into those neptunium mines on E Centauri for a long while."

"Yes, I know that. But I thought that Lortud was pretty safe in spite of the dim view the Earth Council takes of family ownership in things like that. That was one of the reasons he accepted command of this expedition, wasn't it? To help prove that he wasn't just being idle rich, and was competent in addition to being public-spirited?"

"That's right," said Pelham. "But there's a catch in it. I was talking to him just the other day. He's worried for fear the corporations will go before the Council and ask them to make the mines public property on the ground that there isn't anyone to manage them. That is, if he stays away too long."

"Hm-m," said Eschelman. "They're trying to get him coming and—— Yes?"

A messenger was inside the door with one of the blue forms in his hand. Eschelman took it and glanced at the signature. "Too bad you didn't take me on that bet, Captain," he said. "This is the *Impero* reporting with her plot of the course. . . . Wait a minute, though." He stepped to the calculator, picked up the tape, and compared it with the figures on the message, then picked up the intercom instrument. "Communications? Take a message: 'Commander Eschelman to Commander Vivaldi, Navigator, *Impero:* Your plotted course disapproved. Fix on some other star than Vega, which is too large. Your course would have probable error of two minutes, fifteen seconds.'"

He turned to the captain. "Those Italians! If we came into the Asmara system with an error like that it would probably take us a week or two of running on rockets to hit the place after coming out of superspeed. Ah, here comes another one. Let's hope this one is right."

"Keep them honest," said the captain. "I've got to go up to the con and take care of my own troubles."

One by one the ships reported and dropped out of the orbiting formation around the *Massachusetts* that made the squadron look like an outsize model of a sodium atom to string out in a long line behind the flagship. Down in the spin-rooms the engineers set the subnuclear motors for automatic operation at superspeed, and the line of ships bounced like tennis balls as they tested in brief spurts of power. A messenger tapped at the door of Lortud's cabin. "Sir, the captain says that all ships have reported ready except the *Southern Cross* and he expects her any minute."

"Very well. Tell him I'll be right up."

In the con the hammocks that would hold officers and men during the first jerk of superspeed were already in position and the pressure turned on. One of the periscope plates showed a picture of blazing Ilya far below, wrapped in an atmosphere of smoke through which still jutted occasional tongues of angry flame; Ilya's sun blazed just at one side of it in this view and the dimmer was on.

Lortud glanced at the picture, shook his head slightly, and turned to Pelham. "Ready on your side?" he asked.

"All departments ready."

"How about you, Yurka?"

"One hand in Battle Station Eleven showing slight symptoms of melancholia. We'll have to watch him when we come out, but I think he'll be all right."

The con talker turned around. "Sir, the *Southern Cross* reports ready for superspeed."

"Very well." Lortud glanced at the chronometer. "Ten minutes." He climbed lightly into the hammock and began buckling its pressure units around him, as Captain Pelham spoke into the general annunciator: "All hands. All hands. We will pass into superspeed at 1552. Superspeed at 1552."

There was a flurry of activity as the others sought their hammocks. "See you in heaven, Shep," called one of the hands to another, and the talker, with his mike still on his face in the hammock, began to announce: "Four minutes to go. Three and a half minutes to go. Three minutes to go. . . . Sixty seconds—fifty-nine—fifty-eight . . . four—three—two—one——"

Captain Pelham's finger jabbed home on the button, and everyone felt the familiar jerk of pain as consciousness left them amid a shower of pinwheeling comets.

III

☐ "I know it's irrational and I ought to turn myself over to Yurka for treatment for pathological worrying," said Lortud, "but this stage always bothers the hell out of me."

Pelham did not turn from the periscope plate he was watching. "I don't see why," he said. "There couldn't be anything much more restful than a couple of weeks spent in a state of virtual non-existence, with nothing but gray on the plates and nothing to do but eat and sleep."

Yurka laughed. "That's just the point, Captain. Super-speed gives the commodore a chance to return to a foetal plane of existence, without responsibilities, and he resents being recalled to reality. It's a very simple matter in psychology."

Lortud made a gesture of irritation. "No, it isn't. That damned non-existence is a bore, if you want to know. I don't have your interest in the imaginary conquests one makes at a chessboard. I want something real to fight."

"A throwback," said Yurka.

"Call it anything you want to. What worries me is what would happen if two of those ships came out of super into the same space. It would be worse than being rammed by an Ilyan."

Yurka pointed at the plate. "There comes one that's safe, anyway," he said, indicating where one of the great balls bobbed across the field of vision and then smoothed out on her course as the rocket jets were turned on. "Which one is she?"

"*Bayern,*" said Pelham. "You can always tell her by those exterior shutters on the side ports. They're supposed to be automatic, but I wouldn't trust them myself."

"That makes seven," said Lortud.

The con talker spoke. "Sir, Communications has a message from the *Impero*. She reports safe arrival from superspeed and is on the other side of that small moon."

"Have Communications tell her to join formation," said Lortud. "I think in view of the fact that it's a semiclosed planet I'll take the *Massachusetts* down first while the others form a cover circle. You never can tell what you're going to run into. We'll cruise in for a landing on the day side, at the shore of one of those seas. We can pick up the water directly, while we're negotiating. We haven't any charts on this place, have we?"

Pelham said, "No. When a planet applies for closed status the Council only issues charts to diplomatic craft. But it seems normal enough from this distance, except that those polar caps are rather small and there doesn't seem to be much cloud in the atmosphere. Maybe they have a water shortage themselves."

"*Miyako* reports in, sir," said the talker.

"You might call Eschelman and ask him to look up the other planets in this system, just in case of emergency," said Lortud.

"I've already done that," said Pelham. "They're not much use. Number One is a dust planet, with no water. Number Two's too small; lost most of its atmosphere. Four and Five are methane. If we don't strike it rich here we'll have to go find us another system."

Lortud's lips tightened. "By God, we better get what we need here! I'm not going to go wandering all over the universe——"

The talker said, "Sir, Communications reports the *Chacabuco* and *Gloire* have arrived safely from superspeed."

"Very well," said Lortud. "That leaves only one." He picked up the intercom. "Communications? As soon as the remaining ship joins, send out an all-squadron signal for a ring formation with the flag at the center. I intend to make a slow descent on the daylight side of this planet for the purpose of landing. They are to maintain ring formation above, five miles in atmosphere, or as much lower as necessary for close observation. Six battle stations on each ship to be manned; emergency watches in all power rooms until canceled by signal." He turned to the others. "I'm going up to the bubble. Want to come with me, Yurka?"

As the door closed behind the pair of lieutenant wearing the gold shoulder cord of the Officer of the Day said, "Sir, would you mind explaining something? They taught us at the Academy that that circular formation was awfully weak if you were attacked."

Pelham smiled. "Only if you're attacked in space and from space. You forget that a closed planet is not allowed to have space ships, and Lortud's formation is just the thing against anything coming up from the ground. The commodore remembered; that's how he got to be commodore—by remembering all the factors in the situation."

The ship had been turned so that the two men in the observation bubble could look downward at the surface toward which they were riding, much as though they were in the seats of a helicopter lift. It was shortly after dawn at the spot toward which they were descending; the glare from the braking rockets back in the center of the ship threw a weird, more-than-sunlight brilliance across the tops of stunted trees and a white sand beach that seemed almost waveless.

Yurka said, "Do you know, Commodore, what I'd most like to do when we land? Get out on that beach and have a swim."

"Perhaps it can be arranged," said Lortud. "What do you make of the place so far? I'd say those trees looked like acacias, which would mean a dry climate, fairly hot."

"In this region, yes. Might be a desert area, though. I haven't seen a sign of any cities, or even any buildings."

"There was something among the trees in that range of hills out there, toward galactic east. Looked like an overgrown beehive, but it was big enough to be about the size of a cathedral. What I don't see is any signs of animal life; not even birds."

The annunciator clicked and spoke: "All hands. Laboratory reports air 8 per cent high in nitrogen content, 14 point 2 per cent deficient in water vapor. Gravity, point 84. No apparatus necessary, but landing parties should take precautions against overexertion."

Below, the tops of some of the trees suddenly began to shrivel in the rocket blast. Lortud picked up the intercom. "Pelham? Yurka and I will make a landing from the port below the bubble, and see what the score is. Equip a landing party with side arms to accompany us, and break out a helicopter lift in case we don't make contact. You might also start taking water at once and if there's no sign of interference, call in the *Invincible* and *Impero* to do the same. They're the shortest on water."

The *Massachusetts* touched the ground with a gentle bump, rocked once or twice, and settled into the nest she had dug for herself. From below the bubble there was a clamor of equipment and the sound of feet along the passages. Both men felt suddenly lighter as the ship's artificial gravity went off and was replaced by the lesser attraction of the planet.

"Let's go," said Lortud and led the way to the port compartment, where the detail of ten was already waiting, gas and rocket pistols strapped to their sides. A bright-eyed cadet saluted smartly. The air lock closed with a hiss of pressure. "All right, Kocynski," said Lortud. "Lower away."

The cadet swung the handle of the indicator; with a clank of machinery the compartment was lowered to the ground, tilting slightly with the unevenness beneath, and as Lortud swung the lever the door slid back to release them on Asmara.

It had been a good landing, not thirty feet from the water's edge, which they were facing. To the left, the acacialike trees followed around the curve of the shore and ran back up a slight slope in a many-armed tangle. The sand was firm underfoot but showed no footprints or other markings. There was no wind, and not a sound anywhere except the rattle at the port of the ship, where a suction hose was emerging and being directed toward the water's edge by invisible hands from within.

"Spooky sort of place, isn't it?" said Yurka. "Doesn't seem to be overpopulated."

"That's the whole point of colonial planets," said Lortud. "What's that?" He pointed, then strode toward and picked out of the sand a black object from which dangled thin bones. "Looks like the skeleton of a snake, but there isn't any head."

"Maybe somebody——" began Yurka, but was interrupted by a squawk from the lowered landing compartment and a loud-hailer voice which shouted, "Commodore Lortud! *Aquidaban* reports slow-flight, large-size aircraft approaching from the south, probably helicopter."

"Who's the talker?" asked Lortud, and as the hand stepped forward with his mike to his lips, said, "Lortud to Pelham: I will receive natives. Bring *Invincible* down and have her start taking water. Belay that helicopter lift for us, though. If these people are going to make the contact I won't need it."

The talker repeated the message, listened attentively for a moment, and then said, "Sir, the ship reports that the water is fresh with a small amount of strontium salt."

"That doesn't mean anything. Just acknowledge. All right, Kocynski. Get your men spread out to cover us, except for this talker, and if you have to shoot, shoot to kill. I'll give you a hand signal. Yurka, you stay with me; I may need your help in interpreting these people's reactions."

A shadow fled across the beach as the huge round bulk of the *Invincible* settled slowly into position beyond the *Massachusetts*, the acacialike vegetation bursting into brief flame at the touch of her blasts. The landing party spread out, some behind the landing compartment, others among the edges of the trees, and there was a wild amount of swearing as they discovered that the acacias had thorns.

"There it comes!" said Yurka, and pointed. Far down the beach, picked out against the cloudless blue sky, a speck grew in size. It approached with a curious buzzing, flylike motion; Lortud gazed at it under a shielding hand. "Well I'll be damned!" he said. "It's both an ornithopter and a helicopter. Some of these colonial races come up with the niftiest ideas."

Yurka said, "I'm not so sure this is good. It might indicate a regressive culture pattern."

"You mean because ornithopters are fundamentally inefficient as powered vehicles? Nuts; you psychs would build a theory out of anything. Get practical."

The whirring and flapping monstrosity came lower, circled once around the *Massachusets*, appeared to notice the three visitors on the beach, and buzzed to a landing a hundred yards or more away. It was at least thirty feet long. A door in its side opened, a set of steps was let down, and someone within rolled a piece of red carpet down the steps. Lortud started forward. "No, wait," said Yurka. "Better psychology to make them come to us."

The occupants of the plane seemed in no particular hurry to do that, but after a few minutes in which there seemed to be stirrings behind the windows of the craft a procession began to emerge.

It was headed by an extremely tall Negro with a fudge of chin whisker, dressed in a long white mantle, embroidered in brilliant color. On his head he wore something like a fur-decked pope's tiara, and he advanced slowly with high, prancing steps, looking down his nose. Behind him came two more, only slightly less elaborately rigged out; around the arms of one coiled an enormous snake, whose head he was holding. The other carried an uplifted sword. Behind them in turn came a little parade of men carrying short rifles, two and two.

"Formalists," breathed Yurka. "This is definitely not good."

"Shut up," said Lortud out of the side of his mouth.

The leader of the group advanced to within a few paces, held up his hand, and began to speak, in a sonorous outpouring of syllables.

"What the hell is he saying?" said Lortud. "I can't understand a word."

"That's what happens when a planet is closed for a few hundred years," said Yurka. "They develop local dialects. Wait a minute, though."

He took a step forward and lifted his own hand. "Please repeat more slowly," he said, then over his shoulder to the commodore, "He's talking Universal all right. It's just that it sounds queer. If you watch his lips you can get the form of the words."

The tall Negro raised his hand again and spoke more slowly. "In the name of the Most High God Mashasha and Zauditu whose blood is life-giving water, I command you to depart from the planet of the Kaicones, which is closed to exterior contacts. I am Ras Tekla Giorgis."

Lortud said slowly, "I am Commodore Lortud of the Earth Squadron in United Planets Punitive Fleet 14. We are in distress for lack of provisions and water, and will pay for what we need."

Ras Tekla Giorgis raised his hand again. "The children of the Most High God Mashasha are forbidden to accept unclean articles produced on planets not under his blessing. For know you, that the unclean universe and all that is made in it shall vanish away in a moment, in a puff of flame, and we will not suffer ourselves to be contaminated."

"Oh, my God," murmured Yurka, "religious fanatics."

Lortud said, "It's contrary to the laws of the Council of United Planets to refuse help to any ship in distress. And we're an official squadron."

The hand went down and came up again. "This Council also is of the unclean, and shall pass away. The Most High God Mashasha forbids us to contaminate ourselves to obey its laws."

Yurka saw a vein begin to swell at the edge of the commodore's forehead. He put a hand on Lortud's arm. "Let me try," he said and, stepping forward, lifted his own hand.

"Ras Tekla Giorgis, would it not spread the light of your most high god farther in the universe if materials produced under his hands were carried to other worlds?"

The idea appeared to strike him as new. He turned and whispered for a moment to the pair with the sword and snake, then turned back. "No," he said. "For know you, that all that is on this planet is the body of the Most High God Mashasha, or the blood of the Goddess Zauditu. And if part of their being were separated from them at the moment of the coming of the flame they would suffer intolerable agonies."

"Look here," said Lortud, and flung a pointing hand toward the *Massachusetts*. "This is a warship. It carries guns and rockets that shoot. Now if you're going to get technical about this, so am I. I want some provisions and water for my ships or I'm going to take them." He swung to the talker, but before he could give an order one of the Kaicone soldiers ran forward, grasping his leader's arm, babbling excitedly, and pointing to where the ship's intake hose was being coiled in, spilling splashes of water on the bright sand.

"They steal the blood of Zauditu!" bellowed the Ras. "They are birds!"

The man with the snake gave a shout, knelt down on the sand, and stretched out its head; the man with the sword gave another shout, swung his blade up, and with one stroke severed the reptile's head.

Somebody shouted something like "Malala!" "Down!" cried Lortud, and Yurka found himself knocked flat as a missile zinged ominously over him to burst with a roar against the *Massachusetts'* side. Lortud had his pistol out; it sissed as he let go a rocket charge and the man with the sword collapsed, a flame bursting from his middle. The Ras was down, too, his tiara jumping across the sand where it was struck by a miss.

The air seemed filled with projectiles, bursting in bright spots of flame where they struck. The men of the landing party were crisscrossing the beach with their shots, running a pace or two and dropping to fire again while the Kaicone soldiers raked the entrance to the landing compartment. Then, with a tremendous double BOOM! something arched from behind the trees and struck the topside of the *Massachusetts* in a burst of liquid flame.

"Back in!" bellowed Lortud. "They've got a thermite gun there!"

A shadow flashed past as one of the Earth ships above circled toward where the shot had come from. Then the little group were inside and the door clanging shut, one man slumping across the threshold and another whimpering slightly as he gripped a hand that had been mashed to a stump.

"All here?" demanded Lortud.

"Lost three," panted Cadet Kocynski. "Couldn't do anything for them. They were hit by explosives."

"Lift away," ordered the commodore. As the compartment rose, it rang to the shock of two more explosive bullets and little dents appeared in the side.

IV

☐ "All right, Purdy," said Lortud. "I want that report to go on special space transmission to the Council at once. Then you can feel around the local band and if there's anything in this region, give it to them, too, as an information broadcast. I don't imagine there will be, though, outside of something under superspeed."

"What I'd like to do is go down there and blow those fellows apart," said Pelham hardly.

"We'll be lucky if they don't hold us blamable as it is," said Lortud a trifle grimly. "The general rule of the Council is that the outsider is always wrong."

"Yes," said Yurka. "We quite clearly violated one of their religious taboos in taking water. By the way, did you notice that old harpy yelled we were birds just before he gave the signal for opening fire by chopping off the snake's head? I'll bet birds never developed there, and they only have the word."

"I didn't see any insects either," said Lortud. "But that doesn't mean much. We weren't there long enough, and we were in the early morning, which is the wrong time of day for insects anyway. But that reminds me; I think I'll make a supplemental report, asking for an investigation of local conditions, including customs. It's all right for a planet to close up when it wants to develop its individual culture, but the rest of us should at least be informed as to what goes on. I'm not a bit happy about making for another semiclosed planet after that experience, and I have half a mind to run for home on what supplies we have."

"The *Impero's* very low on water and the *Miyako* is getting there," said Pelham, "and most of the other ships have spent some during the trip to Asmara."

"We have full tanks now, and the *Invincible* nearly. We could beef them up and cut the protein ration."

Yurka said, "I'm afraid I couldn't consent to that, Commodore. Aside from the fact that the medics will tell you that insufficient protein will make the men physically inefficient, you'd have half a dozen cases of various kinds of neuroses on your hands within three days after cutting protein. That's the Gaynor reaction and there isn't anything better established in space psychology."

Lortud growled in his throat. "I could make it an order. I'm commander of this squadron, and it wasn't organized to hunt for pork chops for the crews, dammit! You faith healers make me sick!"

Yurka said, "You can order anything you wish in the squadron, sir, but I'm afraid psychological reactions aren't under orders."

"All right, dammit! I wasn't arguing with you." He picked up the intercom. "Navigation? Is Eschelman there? Oh, off watch. Well, Holmgren, suppose you start the job of setting a course for Kushan—yes, the semiclosed planet over in the region of Ras Algethi that we were looking up before we came to this condemned place." He punched the buttons again. "Communications? An all-ship signal: set a course for Kushan, report to Commander Eschelman for master computation. No hurry on it; we can't go into super until you send that report in and get an acknowledge."

Yurka said, "Would it cause an unreasonable delay if I sent in a report too? I think a danger point is apt to develop if closed and semiclosed planets are allowed to work up a degree of religious fanaticism such as we ran into down there. They're trying to keep everybody out, but it just might twist around to the point where they wanted to take other planets in."

"Thinking of another infection like that on Ilya, eh?" said Lortud. "All right, write your report and I'll endorse it. I don't think it will do you any good, though, with the Council as determined as it is to let cultures develop along their own lines."

The talker said, "Sir, the *Gloire* asks if you need a repair party for the damage caused by that thermite shell. They have a heavy reserve of asterite steel."

Lortud glanced at Pelham. The captain said, "Tell them no, thanks. We've inspected and it was low-grade thermite, the old-fashioned kind and not radioactive. Looks ugly but not much damage."

Lortud said, "I'm going to my cabin. Have me called when we're ready for the jump."

With a jerk the timeless gray of superspeed on the periscope screens gave place to the flaming yellow of star H.D. 99571. Brilliant as Venus and as shrouded in cloud, the planet Kushan loomed dead ahead. Pelham swung the engine indicator to "Rockets—Slow" and remarked, "Nice job of navigation. Right on the nose. You can call the commodore."

Yurka said, "What I don't understand about him . . ." and stopped.

"What is it?" asked Pelham.

"Never mind now. I was just thinking about something that didn't add up during the superspeed run. But a psychological officer shouldn't talk until he has a clear case."

Pelham turned and looked at him. "Do you mean——"

Yurka nudged him just as Lortud came through the door and simultaneously the talker announced, "*Dent Ardent* reports in, sir."

The commodore stepped to the screens and glanced

over what they showed. "Didn't know it had a cloud cover," he said. "They ought to put those things in the catalogue. Yeoman!"

"Yes, sir."

"Take down the following, to be sent out by Communications as soon as the circuits are clear. 'All-ships signal: formation for approaching planet will be arrow, *Massachusetts* leading, *Impero* immediately behind, *Louisiana* and *Chacabuco* as flankers'—they're the best gunnery ships, but you needn't put that in the signal—'rest to follow in order of arrival. Maintain visual contact. *Impero* to follow *Massachusetts* in when flagship lands and begin taking water immediately, but without discharging landing party until signaled by flag.' That's all."

The lieutenant who had asked about the circular formation as they approached Asmara gazed admiringly at the broad back as Lortud went through the door on his way to the bubble. "How does he do it?" he said. "I wouldn't have figured out that approach on a suspicious planet with cloud cover in three hours."

"Hmpf," said the cadet who was operating the screens. "You would if your name were Alstair Lortud. We were figuring out in junior mess yesterday that he's spent more time in space than on Earth, and this is his fourth punitive expedition."

Down in the bubble Lortud and Yurka watched the shining clouds drift up until they were surrounded by a dazzle so bright it hurt the eyes. The reports came through steadily; gravity a trifle above Earth's, high percentage of water vapor in an atmosphere otherwise normal, strong wind currents, *Bayern* at the center of the column reporting difficulty maintaining visual contact on her next ahead and requesting permission to use radar.

Suddenly they were through the cloud blanket and angling in on a landscape all round, verdant hills and broad rivers that twisted together toward a distant sea, over which there were streaks of rain.

"Cities here all right," Yurka said, and pointed to where, under the curiously diffused and shadowless light, like that in an operating room, two of the rivers came together. All the point of land where they joined was covered with what were evidently human structures, and a tracery of bridges ran across the streams to join other collections of buildings.

Lortud turned to the intercom. "Con? Make landing in that hollow at the edge of the smaller stream, just to galactic north of the city. Drop the tail-end ship back for high cover. Others over the city, intervaled out, at eight miles, except *Impero*."

He turned back to watch the growing city. There were few straight lines in it, either vertical or in the plan of the streets. The annunciator clicked and pronounced: "Laboratory says this planet has a slow rotation and thirty-five-hour day, approx."

Lortud clicked an answer. "Very well. Yurka and I will land as before. Have a landing party ready, but you needn't man more than three battle stations. A race with that size and type of permanent structures will be awfully careful about starting anything rough."

The *Massachusetts* began to rock gently. Yurka chuckled. "Our staff captain is no fool," he said. "He's noticed the culture down there, too, and is using his side blasts, being careful about smashing things below."

"Let's be ready," said Lortud, without answering directly, and led the way to the exit compartment. The detail entered it a moment later; the ship touched ground with a lurch that almost threw them off their feet and caused Lortud to say something profane under his breath about being too damn careful of causing damage on landing, and they were lowered to the ground.

As the door opened a wave of dank heat seemed to

flow over them. The brilliant, shadowless light showed they were stepping out into lush grass, some hundred yards from the bank of the river. One of the landing party slapped suddenly at his face, and Lortud turned and grinned. "Don't worry," he said. "The bite won't poison you, or the planet wouldn't be declared habitable."

He led the way through ankle-deep grass that squished under the feet up a slope toward where a row of heavy-leaved trees extended broad arms in a pattern too regular to be the work of nature alone. "Ouch!" said Yurka, and slapped in turn. "Commodore, these insects may not be poisonous, but I'll take a nice earthly mosquito."

They reached the crest. Behind the line of trees was a road—or what had been a road, for the surface of compacted crushed stone was mostly worn away, and there were deep ruts with muddy bottoms. Beyond it a once white building, tumble-down and stained, presented a vacant face, and a small pink animal scuttled away into rank growths.

Lortud gazed around. "Welcome to Kushan," he said. "The committee seems to be delayed. All right—what's your name? Brashear? You may as well get your men posted along those trees."

Yurka slapped again. "If I were an archaeologist instead of a psychologist," he said, "I think I'd call this an animal-transport road. And I'm not sure I like that any better than the signs of regressive culture on Asmara."

"Phew, it's hot," said Lortud, and turned round to watch the *Impero* settle neatly into her berth beyond their own ship. "Well, if they have animal transport they have animals, and animals are protein. In fact there comes one now."

Over the hill from the direction of the city Yurka saw a large, dun-colored creature approaching at a placid walk, dragging behind it an extraordinary vehicle that looked like a parody of one of the early Earth automobiles found in museums. It ambled slowly toward the three men who stood waiting. Lortud told the talker, "Tell them we have apparent contact."

As it drew near it was evident that the strange vehicle was decorated with streamers in many colors, most of them faded or stained. A man in the front seat of the vehicle controlled the beast by a pair of cords leading to its mouth. He drew up beside the visitors from space, called something to the animal which caused it to stand, and leaped to the ground.

He was small, with a dark skin, and a smile that seemed engraved upon his pleasant face. As soon as he was facing the visitors he put one hand over his eyes, bowed deeply, and in an accent almost as unintelligible as that of the Kaicones said, "Lords from outer worlds, I am devoured with regrets, but I am required to inform you that this is a semiclosed planet, and we cannot receive your commerce."

Lortud said, "We're not establishing relations. This is a squadron of a United Planets punitive force, a battle squadron. All we want is some water and provisions. I am Commodore Lortud of Earth."

The man bowed again. "And I am your slave, Vijanam Adhel of the Kshastra race of Kushan. Lord, we have utmost reverence for the authorities of the United Planets, and all that we have is yours. Will you do me the pleasure to accompany me before our high citizens that we may the better minister to you?"

The talker said, "Sir."

Lortud turned. "What is it?"

"A message from the *Impero*, sir. They request permission to land. They have several natives outside, making friendly signs."

The brown man bowed again. "Lord," he said, "if you have others of your company, will you honor us by allowing us to provide them with entertainment and food?"

Lortud wrinkled his brow and said rapidly to the talker,

"Permission granted for a party of ten. Join us here, as escort. Remainder of *Impero* crew not to be over five hundred meters from ship."

Vijanam Adhel said, "Warrior lord, I offer you the apology of Kushan for not attending you with an escort to do you honor and suitable transportation, but this is the hour of our afternoon when all cease from labor to take sweet repose. But if you will indeed accept our hospitality while we discuss the question of how your needs shall be met, I will at once summon cars to spare the weariness of your limbs."

"Okay," said Lortud. "Go ahead."

Vijanam Adhel produced from his shapeless garments something that looked like a diminutive panpipe and passed it rapidly across his lips, blowing into it. "Supersonics," said Yurka in a low voice. "Maybe it will be all right after all, even if they're regressive on transportation. We haven't anything like that."

Vijanam Adhel bowed again. "Lord, your permission to sit." Without waiting for it, he squatted cross-legged into the damp, yielding grasses.

Lortud turned. "Brashear!" he shouted. "Get your men together. You can stay outside the ship if you wish, but don't go more than five hundred meters. The Italians are furnishing me an escort to go to town."

V

☐ The procession of animal-drawn cars stopped before a building whose door pillars were elaborately inlaid with a mosaic in bits of colored enamel, many of which had broken away. Vijanam Adhel climbed out, stood before the door, and whistled. After a minute the door opened slowly on a man who moved languidly forward to the beast's head.

"They're as like each other as so many Chinese," said Lortud in a low voice, "and they all seem to be young."

Yurka said, "And I don't like it any better than Asmara. Commodore, there's something wrong. Have you noticed that everything is dirty or run down? Watch your step."

"For what?" said Lortud, but before the psychological officer could answer, their guide was bowing them into the building which was evidently the Kushanian idea of a palace. They were led through an oval entrance hall with a tessellated floor, through another small room, and found themselves in a big round room with tall windows through which the calm light of Kushan drifted. Around the walls were piles of cushions, on which were reclining a group of men very much like Vijanam Adhel in appearance. They smiled amiably at the Earthmen, but hardly moved except to take from the low tables before them pieces of bright-colored fruit or tall glasses of some kind of wine.

Vijanam Adhel led Lortud and Yurka across the circle toward a fat man with a little whiskbroom of feathers in his headcloth, placed one hand before his face and said that this was the Most Exalted Kshaster of the city of Chandarabad. Lortud brought forward the Italians and introduced them—Captain Cavagnaro, Dr. Antoniotti, Commander Bellino, and the rest. The Most Exalted Kshaster said, "It has reached my ears that you are warrior lords from the mother planet, in need of certain things that we are only too happy to supply. But it is our well-established custom that during the hours of afternoon we take our ease among the delights of our fruit and wine, the better to meet later cares. We pray you to join us in this relaxation."

He waved a languid hand. The visitors, following his motion with their eyes, saw that new piles of cushions had been placed and servants were putting before them low tables, with plates of colored fruits and flagons of wine, like those before the others in the room. Lortud said, "We thank you. We are anxious to return to our home, but I suppose an hour or so won't hurt us."

He led the way toward one of the piles of cushions. The enervating moist heat made the rest seem good. Lortud leaned toward Yurka and said, "There isn't a woman in the place."

"That's all right," said the psychological officer. "This is an Indian colony and they probably have the ancient purdah."

The Kshaster leaned a little toward them. "Lords," he said, "it is decorous and delightful to observe the ceremony of the fruit." He selected a pastel green fruit, picked up a glass-bladed knife, cut out a section, and placed it on his tongue; then took a mouthful of wine and began to chew. A beatific expression spread across the Kshaster's face; his eyes almost closed, and the visitors were aware of a pungent, slightly spicy odor which seemed to come from neither fruit nor wine, but the combination of the two.

As the visitors addressed themselves to similar fruits Yurka said, "Commodore. Something."

"What is it?"

"How did this bird know where we were from and what we wanted? That guide has been with us all the time, and we've just been introduced."

Lortud frowned. "I think it must be that supersonic whistle, not mind reading or anything of that kind. I wish we knew how to operate those things."

He placed his segment of fruit on his tongue and was just about to pick up the glass of wine when there was a shout of "No!" from the cushions on his right. He turned to see Dr. Antoniotti of the Italian ship spit violently, then cut another piece of fruit and crush it into the wineglass.

"What's the matter?" asked Lortud.

"Don't touch it," said the doctor. "It's doped." He took three quick steps toward Lortud and held the wineglass out. "Smell that!"

"Smells rather pleasant. What is it?"

"I wouldn't know everything that's in it, but there's a high concentration of narceine for one thing. Habit-forming and fairly deadly narcotic alkaloid. Good God, look at the captain!"

Cavagnaro had evidently finished his dosage of the combination. He lay back among the cushions, a foolish smile of pleasure spreading across his countenance; beside him, Commander Bellino was sitting upright, but with his mouth open and eyes staring at vacancy. Another of the officers was wagging his bent head back and forth with the slow beat of a metronome.

"So that's it!" said Lortud. He turned fiercely on the Kshaster, hand on his pistol butt. "You'd better explain why you're doping us and make it good and make it fast." He swung to the talker. "Repeat everything to the ship. Number One readiness."

The fat man merely lolled among his cushions, eyes narrowed to slits; his voice came slowly and as though from far away: "Lord, we are but sharing with you the highest of our pleasures. Come rest awhile from every care."

"He's right," said Yurka. "They think they're doing us a favor by letting us in on this mass sleigh ride." He shuddered. "Now I know what's wrong with this place. It's become a planet of drug addicts."

Dr. Antoniotti said, "It must be the combination of that 'wine' with the fruit that releases the narceine. Wonder how they hit on it?"

"I don't know, and I don't care," said Lortud. "Let's get out of here. Talker, ask the ship to break out a helicopter lift and coach it in at the door of this place."

He stood up in a single lithe motion and stepped over to the stricken captain of the Italian ship, who tried to beat him off with feeble hands, still smiling foolishly. Yurka managed to get one of the stricken officers into movement, Antoniotti took another. Vijanam Adhel was wringing his hands and weeping. "Lords, lords, I implore you to visit your hardest punishments on my unworthy head. I am only a messenger, but I assure you that the Kshastra will do anything you desire to recover their place in the affections of the parent race." Lortud growled.

Back aboard the *Massachusetts*, the conference of captains on mutual visual was serious. The status reports showed that practically every ship would have a protein deficiency for any voyage that would take over eight weeks on superspeed.

"That gives us approximately a four-week trip without cutting the reserves down so far that we'd have to drift and ask for a relief supply ship," said Lortud. "I don't imagine any of you want that."

No one felt the need of answering; the last squadron that had gone into drift was Sorenson's of Punitive 7, and all knew too well that every officer in it down to the rank of major had been broken.

"All right, then," Lortud continued. "I just wanted to be sure that none of you would turn in a protest report on me for not doing it. Now we'll consider the other possible plans. Captain Westmorland has suggested that we put out landing parties on some of the less civilized parts of Kushan—if any part of it can really be called civilized—and take some of the local animals by old-fashioned hunting methods. The plan has a certain attractiveness, but it is open to the objection that we might not get enough proteins to pay for our time."

The panel below the pictured face of Westmorland of the *Triumph* clicked to show that he wished to speak. "I don't agree," he said. "With modern weapons——"

Lortud clicked back at him. "There's a more serious objection still," he said. "Dr. Antoniotti of the *Impero* took some of the fruits aboard and analyzed them. He reports their chemistry is such that not only narceine but various other alkaloid narcotics form very readily on contact with liquids containing even small quantities of acids. Now there are small amounts of acid in most animals' bodies. That is, any meat we obtained on Kushan would be apt to be doped. If we had all the time in the world we could search around until we got hold of something drug-free. But time is precisely what we lack. I have therefore decided that we should travel farther."

Westmorland's panel clicked again. "I withdraw my objection," he said.

"Good," said Lortud. "The next question is what direction we shall take. Unfortunately stars with viable planets are comparatively rare in this region. However,

Commander Hondschoote of the *Dent Ardent* has proposed an ingenious solution for our difficulties. He suggests that we make for 221 Serpens, H.D. 87433, which has a planet named Hauraki that is a member of the United Planets organization."

Captain Viollet of the *Gloire* clicked. "What kind of colony is it?" he asked. "We don't want to risk another one where they don't eat proteins."

"It's a secondary colony," explained Lortud. "The original Earth stock came from New Zealand and settled on Roha, in the 21 Ophiucus system. Hauraki was colonized by a group of scientists who didn't want to be bothered with social problems or the arts."

"Just a minute." It was old Captain Salazar of the *Aquidaban*, so famous throughout the fleet for his memory that he was called "The Storage Bank." "As I remember it, Hauraki is nearly seven weeks from here on superspeed, and it's in the wrong direction to take us home."

Lortud smiled. "Right. That's the ingeniousness of Commander Hondschoote's plan. If you will look up your star catalogue you will find that a little less than halfway to Hauraki there's a planet attached to a sun numbered as H.D. 92111, G-type star. It's a red dot planet, that is, with non-humanoid inhabitants, but it is listed as having great quantities of animal life. We can stop there; if we get what we want the stop at Hauraki need only be a friendly visit, and if we don't, we can at least drift near Hauraki."

The row of pictured faces on the panel showed expressions indicating both that the idea was new and that no one could think of any objection precise enough to be put in words. Lortud gave them a minute or two, then:

"Very well. My decision is that we will pass into superspeed for H.D. 92111 at 1030: 71ZX galactic time. Have your navigators chart courses on that basis and report them in for master computation. That will give us a sixteen-hour period in which to discover any objections to the plan and at the same time allow us to start the jump during a morning watch, when it will be more convenient. Conference closes."

He snapped off the communicator. "I don't think there'll be any real objection," said Captain Pelham, and turned toward the door, when Yurka saluted formally. "What is it?"

"Sir, I wish to make a confidential report."

"Oh, Lord. I was hoping we wouldn't have to have one of those on this trip. All right, come along."

He led the way to the captain's cabin, said; "Conference; Commander Keller to take command of the ship until relieved," into the intercom, switched off exterior communication, switched on the recording device, and turned to the psychological officer, who had remained stiffly at atention. "Go ahead, Yurka, who's behaving irrationally now?"

Yurka ran the tip of his tongue around his lips. "Sir, I'm afraid it's Commodore Lortud."

"Lortud! Are you sure you don't need a treatment yourself? What's your evidence?"

"The manner in which he has been conducting this search for food and water. We could have hunted for proteins at Asmara, but he didn't think of that until we got to Kushan, where hunting wouldn't do us any——"

"Just a minute," said Pelham. "Neither Westmorland nor anyone else made any such suggestion at Asmara. Those people have aircraft, thermite guns, and rocket bullets and were determined not to let us have anything that came from their planet. To have gone any farther there would have involved us in military operations against an independent culture, which is strictly contrary to interplanetary law. You know that as well as I do."

"Yes, Captain. It isn't any one incident, but the continuing pattern we have to deal with in space psychology. And I'm not suggesting that his spot-command judgment has been affected. It's the over-all planning."

Pelham touched his mustache. "Go on. Where's your pattern?"

"He was very anxious to get from Asmara to Kushan, which didn't bring us any nearer home. Now he's just as anxious to get away from Kushan in a direction that will take us right away from Earth, and with a stopover at a planet whose characteristics are altogether uncertain."

"But that wasn't his plan; it came from Commander Hondschoote on the *Dent Ardent*."

"He accepted it at once."

Pelham brought down a hand. "Look here, are you suggesting that the commodore doesn't want to get home soon? Because if you are, I'd say you were irrational instead of him. There isn't a man in the squadron who has more reason to get back quick, or who has shown more anxiety to do so. We were talking about it just the other day."

"That can be explained in psychology. He has every desire to get back, but at the same time he's dealing with an overwhelming subconscious compulsion against it, trying to fight off the compulsion. That's the reason for the difference between his words and actions. It might even be an induced compulsion, something that went wrong with his conditioning. I've heard of such cases."

There was a moment's silence as Pelham considered. Then he shook his head slowly. "No, Yurka, I won't buy it. In the first place the idea came from Hondschoote. He's the best navigator in the squadron, and if there were any planet more directly on the route to Earth that we could reach with the supplies we have, he'd know about it. In the second place, you were monitoring that conference yourself, and you saw that none of the captains objected to the plan or even made countersuggestions. Your theory requires that not only Lortud should be subject to this compulsion against getting home soon, but all the captains in the fleet. Including myself." He smiled. "If that's irrational, I say let's all be bugs together."

VI

☐ "It might be the old Earth," mused Yurka, looking down at the smooth range of green valley flanked by tall, cliff-sided hills, along which they were flying at some three thousand meters.

"The Earth as it will be when it gets a couple hundred thousand years older and hasn't as many oceans," amended Lortud. "No, that isn't right either. There doesn't seem to be any general lack of water. That vegetation down there is green as it can be, and there are certainly streams. It's just that they're a little short on oceans."

The annunciator buzzed and said, "*Louisiana* to Commodore; We have sighted what is apparently animal life."

Lortud picked up the intercom. "Communications, make a general signal to hover." He changed connections. "Con? Get a big helicopter lift ready, with an armed landing party. I think I'll take Commander Keller with me instead of Yurka. Psychology won't be so much use as someone from the technical end in dealing with non-humanoids. You might also signal to the *Miyako* that she has permission to send down a landing party for samples of non-intelligent life and analyze for protein content. If those Japs can take it, anybody can. They all have delicate stomachs."

He went through the door, buckling on his pistol, and the *Massachusetts* began to bounce slowly, like a languid rubber ball, as the power units went into the hovering routine. "Also he has to take command of every landing party in person," murmured Yurka, gazing after him. "I wish I could identify——"

"Beg pardon?" said a major from the engineering division, who had come up on his off-duty period to get a look at a new world.

"Nothing." He lifted the long-range glass and pointed it downward. "Look. Those must be the animals the *Louisiana* saw, down there to the left. Certainly look like cows at this distance, but we haven't anything to compare them with for size, not knowing how tall that vegetation is."

The big helicopter swung down and settled silently into grasses whose edges were feathered out like giant milfoil. Lortud snapped open the door and stepped out, almost instantly going hip-deep into the vegetation. "Ground's firm enough," he said, and reached a hand up to help Keller, a big, bushy-browed man, who had a minny gun strapped across his back, while the landing detail climbed out the after door of the machine.

"Testing, testing," said the talker.

"There they are." Keller pointed to where, about three hundred yards away, a row of red-brown backs rose above the greenery in a pattern strangely like that of a herd of grazing cattle. "Say, this air sure has sparkle in it."

"It's the extra oxygen," said Lortud. He addressed the detail. "All right, men, spread out in skirmisher formation and guide on me. Those animals are obviously grazers and not any form of intelligent life, and we want one of them. Use bullets, not rocket shells, unless they try to attack."

As the men spread, the *Miyako's* helicopter was visible, drifting in farther down the valley. A flying creature of some kind drifted from the ground, whirled once around it and down again. The pilot of the helicopter leaned out and called, "Shall I keep over you, sir?"

"No," said Lortud, and either the sound of his voice or the movements of the men spreading out in their semicircle seemed to rouse the attention of one of the grazing beasts. It lifted a long, mournful cowlike face and stared at them; there was a single horn, with a curious metallic sheen, in the center of the forehead, and a pair of ears as large as buckets and fantastically involuted. The creature did not seem particularly disturbed by the sight of the Earthmen, merely swung its head from side to side to gaze at one after another, finally fixing on the helicopter, and, opening a wide mouth, emitted a sound like the coo of a gigantic pigeon. It was a little larger than a cow.

"Aim about for the eye," called Lortud. Two of the landing party threw up their weapons almost simultaneously, there were a pair of brief, soundless flashes, and the animal dropped, threshing. The fall of their companion brought up a whole row of heads which, like the first one, gazed at the circling Earthmen and fixed attention on the helicopter. Then, without any appearance of undue alarm, the herd began moving slowly away, heads bobbing at the ends of rather absurdly thin necks.

"I'd say they were domesticated," said Keller. "Presumably by the non-humanoid inhabitants, whoever they are. But I haven't seen any sign of them."

"That's right," said Lortud, pushing through the rank grasses. "Talker, see if you can get the *Miyako's* helix and ask them whether they have any sign of the inhabitants."

Not all the grasses were alike. Some of them had small flowers of a peculiarly intense blue. "*Miyako* party says no, sir," the talker came back. "But they have encircled several specimens of local animals."

Both shots had struck the creature squarely in the eye, and it was quite thoroughly dead. "Beefsteaks!" said one of the party, and there was a little laugh from the others.

Keller bent over to examine it. "I think it is beefsteaks at that," he said. "Look, it has an udder, and I didn't see any young around, so the chances are that the local farmers use milk. No hoofs, though, just splay feet. Hmm."

He bent over and tapped the horn, then took out his knife and tapped it again. It gave off a distinct ring.

"Why, it's metal!" he said. "Wha do you think of that, Commodore?"

Lortud shook his head. "I'm not enough of a biologist to think about it," he said. "If it's good to eat, that's all I ask. Anybody think to bring a protein-testing unit?"

"I did, sir," said the cadet in charge of the landing party, and produced the small box in which foods were chemically sampled.

"All right, take a cut off this animal's rump, and—what is it?"

The talker said, "Sir, the ship reports receiving intense, pulsating radar emanations."

"It does, does it?" said Lortud, turning and gazing around. "Now where in the blue-belted blazes would they be coming from?" He pointed. "Will you look at that, Keller?"

The group of animals that had been moving slowly away from them had broken into a huge, clumsy gallop through the tall grasses and were headed toward the cliffs at the far side of the valley, stumpy tails held high. As the visitors from Earth watched, a section of what had seemed the stone face of the cliff slid upward to reveal a black opening. Lortud whipped up his folding glasses; so did Keller.

"That cliff face is metal!" he cried. "The whole damned thing's a structure!"

"So it is," said Keller, "and the animals are making for it like billy-o."

"Sir," said the cadet, "there seems to be another one of those doors opening. Farther along, there."

Lortud turned swiftly to the talker. "Tell ship to train

on those doorways, load with atomics," he said. "And come down to one thousand. Helicopter, ready to pick us up, emergency. Is anything coming out, Keller?"

"No, they're going in, just like the animals into Noah's ark. There, look; there goes the last one, and the door is starting to come down again."

Lortud lowered his glasses. "Guess they aren't very dangerous after all," he said. "Just wanted to keep their herds away from us, and I can't say I altogether blame them. What do you make of it, Keller?"

"I'd say you were probably right. What interests me is how they called the animals in." He indicated the dead beast with his foot. "You know what I think? I think it's some form of radar. See those ears; they look as though they belonged on overgrown bats. You could receive a lot of radiation with them."

Lortud lifted his glasses and surveyed the cliff again. "I don't see any sign of apparatus," he said. He put one hand to his forehead. "This wants thinking out. I believe you're right about the radar; that must have been what the ship reported. But it can't be very efficient, or they'd have beamed it instead of giving it so wide a spread that the ship picked it up at three thousand meters."

"Not necessarily," said Keller. "It might——"

"Sssh, you're interrupting. Also, pending examination, they have just what we need in the way of proteins. And aside from the fact that it wouldn't be exactly fair to take their property without compensation, it doesn't seem likely that we would get very much of it. Keller, I'm going over there and try to establish relations."

The commander cleared his throat.

"Well? Any objections?"

"Not exactly. But, Commodore, this is a red dot planet."

"Yes, I know—not suitable for human colonization except under military guard and as ordered. But we're the military. Talker, send this: 'Commodore to Captain Pelham: Will attempt to make contact with inhabitants of this planet to secure needed food supplies peaceably. Sending you beef carcass. Investigate biological aspects as well as availability for food.' " He swung round. "Now, you men, this is strictly a volunteer proposition, above and beyond duty. Anybody who wishes can go back to the ship, and I'll skin the man alive who says it isn't an honorable thing to do. Get that helix over here."

It was evidently growing toward late afternoon on Planet 2:92111, with long shadows striking across the valley from tree-covered hills on the side opposite the cliffs. The cadet closed his testing box and said, "The test's negative, sir. No dangerous substances or reactions."

"Good," said Lortud. "Let's go."

He led the way himself, down the slight slope to the bottom where a small stream ran through, and there was swearing and laughter as somebody got a shoeful. The talker said, "*Miyako* reports the beef very edible, sir, and recommends electronic cooking."

"Very well," said Lortud. "Now as we go up this slope toward that door you'd better expand into skirmisher formation again, flankers well forward to give me close cover from under the edge of the cliff. Keller, suppose you drop off here with that minny gun for high-angle cover. As soon as that helix gets away from the ship, coach it in for overhead cover."

He led the way up the slope, where the grass grew less rankly and had been trodden down by the passage of many animal feet. As one approached the cliff, against which the setting sun now struck almost level, it became apparent that its rocklike appearance was due to a series of tapering corrugations in the dull gray metal of its composition. Lortud strode up to it, walked along a few steps in either direction, and tapped. The only answer was a dull ring of metal. "Report to the ship that there doesn't seem to be any means of entry," he told the talker. "Oh, Keller! Come on up here." He motioned in a couple of the detail as well, and the group contemplated the structure.

"The tops of those corrugations, up there, where they flare out, must be air intakes," said the commander. "But what beats me is that there doesn't seem to be anything like a window."

"Yes," agreed Lortud, "and the metal's tremendously heavy. The whole thing is built like a fortress. My guess would be that whoever lives in a place like that has some pretty dangerous natural enemies." He turned to the talker. "Tune up your instrument, son. I want them to hear everything we're saying, so that if anything goes wrong they'll know where to pin the medal."

"Shall I let this door have a blast?" asked Keller.

"Not yet. No use smashing up the furniture until we're sure we can't get in any other way."

He led the way along the top of the slope. The doors seemed to fit so snugly into the surface of the structure that it was impossible to tell where one left off and the other began. The talker said, "Sir, the helicopter lift says that one of the doors is opening, down there ahead."

"Come on!" cried Lortud, and led the group at a run along the line of metal wall. It jutted out in a slight curve. As they came around it there was the opening, the long evening light striking into a cavernous gap some twenty feet high, with a smooth floor leading downward at a slight angle. Somewhere inside there was a faint luminescence, but not enough to make out any detail, and from somewhere near the luminescence came the exaggerated coo of one of the grazing beasts.

"I guess we go in," said Lortud, and pressed forward.

VII

☐ For about a hundred yards the tunnel led straight on, its floor giving the ring of metal. The light was too faint to make out much detail of what lay beyond, except that the passage seemed to divide around a wedgelike projection, with the right-hand wing wholly dark.

"Look out," said one of the men. "Here they come," and the passage behind was abruptly filled with the splat of the grazing animals' feet and the bubbling coo of their voices, as thirty or forty of them came in. The Earthmen pressed against the wall to let them pass; as each one came abreast of the group it turned its curious bat-eared head toward them, emitted a coo or two, then pushed on with the rest, taking the left-hand passage. The leaders of the group were hardly well engaged in it when, with a heavy clang, the outside door came down, and the Earthmen were in almost complete darkness.

Someone swore. Lortud said, "We're in for it now. Someone, make a light. Talker, can you still get the ship?"

The hand said, "No, sir. The normal channels won't work through all that metal."

"Try the low angstrom bands. As soon as they realize we're out of communication they'll probably make a setup in that region, and their excitation will give you power enough to get through an answer. Keller, let's take the turn to the left here. That's where those animals went, and it's them we're after. You better drop back and be rear cover with that minny gun. Levine, you're the point; I'll be right cover and Wallace left, as light man. I don't think we better do any more talking than necessary."

The luminescence, which came from the center of the ceiling, had a curious foglike quality that seemed to cut off the beam of Wallace's light a few feet ahead. Beyond its interruption the left-hand passage curved leftward more sharply still, crossed a metal projection a foot or so from the floor, over which Levine stumbled, and the visitors from Earth found themselves looking at a huge round and domed chamber divided by a partition about shoulder-high. On the near side of it the grazing animals were moving slowly about or lying down; from the far side came cooings, and small animals of the same type stuck up heads to contemplate the visitors.

"It's a stock pen," said someone.

Keller suddenly shouted, "Hey!" and they turned to see coming down the passage a creature as strange as a dream. Fully twelve feet the body reared from the floor, carapaced like that of a lobster, and dully shining in Wallace's light. Two pairs of short jointed legs, moving rapidly, gave its progress the appearance of a trot; there were at least four pairs of other appendages, two of them terminating in parodies of fingers, the others in tentacles that were now carrying big metallic hexagonal boxes that looked like containers of some sort. There was a head with two long pairs of antennae in front of cuplike orifices and a long prognathous jaw, but nothing that could be called a face.

"Ugh!" said someone. The creature stopped, waved its antennae toward the little group of men, opened its mouth, and uttered a series of sounds not too much unlike the cooing of the grazing beasts.

"It's blind," said Keller. "It hasn't got any eyes."

"But it can hear," said Lortud. He stepped forward,

held out a hand in the universal gesture of friendliness, and said, "We come as friends, or as you would perhaps put it, coo, coo, cuddly-coo."

For answer, the creature's head bent forward, both sets of antennae approaching Lortud's head closely; gave a shrill whistle and a series of clicks; dropped one of the metallic boxes and with a tentacled hand explored Lortud's as far up as the cuff of his uniform. This appeared to disconcert it slightly; the tentacles writhed back, the creature said, "Coo, coo, cuddly-coo, tsk, tsk." Then it picked up the box again and pushed on past the Earthmen to the grazing animals.

It placed the box under the udder of one of these, opened it, and began to milk rapidly.

"Seems friendly enough," observed Lortud, "but he's apparently telling us he has to get his chores done before indulging in a taste for society. What do you make of it, Keller?"

"About the same," said the commander. "Did you notice the highly developed speech system, though? It made three or four different classes of sounds. And there's a big brain case. And that business with the antennae. It must have a couple of senses we lack to compensate for sight. It would be fascinating to learn something about that lobster's evolutionary history."

"I'll bet I know what one of those senses is," said Lortud. "It must have something to do with radar. Did you notice how all those grazers flocked in, apparently on call? What I don't understand is how something built on the crustacean scheme could grow that big. The internal-muscle system wouldn't support a creature of that size on any Earth-type planet I know."

Keller said, "You don't know all the details. From what I saw of that beef we killed and what I can see of our friend here, I think that shell is metal, and heavy metal, at that. There's a different physical chemistry at work here."

Lortud swung to the talker, who was still fiddling with his instrument. "Any luck?"

"No, sir, not yet. There seems to be quite a lot of static on some of the bands, but nothing I can make out."

"Keep at it. Maybe some of the senses they have here are electrical. Hello."

Down the passage in the pale fluorescence came another of the lobster men. This one carried a kind of long-handled mallet, whose outer head had a long cutting edge let into it. The creature trotted toward the group of humans, calling "Coo. coo, cuddly-coo," as it came with surprising rapidity.

"Look out!" cried Keller suddenly, and Lortud whipped out his pistol, but even as he fired, the creature brought his weapon down with a crash on the head of Levine. There was a blast of flame where the rocket struck, the lobster man staggered but, apparently uninjured, reached two of its hands down to pick up Levine's body.

"Scatter," shouted Lortud, "and let him have it!"

"Aim for those antennae!" cried Keller.

The landing party spread, ducking to the floor, one even vaulting the partition into the pen that held the calves, and the intolerable crash and flare of rocket bullets filled the cavern as hit after hit burst against the lobster creature's carapace. It wove from side to side under impacts that would have smashed in the side of a house, but neither halted nor went down, and in a moment had disappeared round the turn of the passage.

"My God! My God!" sobbed the cadet. "Poor Levine."

"Shut up," said Lortud savagely, and as he said it the faint light from overhead flicked once and went out.

"Wallace, can you find that partition wall in the dark?"

"Yes, sir."

"All right, get over it and throw your light on that other beast, the one doing the milking. I want to find out how he's taking it."

There was a sound of scrambling, then the beam of light shot out and searched round the pen that held the larger animals. Except for them it was empty.

"They can move fast," said Lortud. "Anybody else have a light?"

"I have, sir," said a voice.

"All right, throw it on me, and I want you men to rally round, so we won't be separated. . . . Now listen, we're up against a tough proposition here. These lobsters evidently regard us as biological specimens or as some form of beef cattle, the way we took their pets here, and they're so well armored we can't hurt them."

"How about gas?" said someone.

"Not in this confined space. I take it nobody brought masks."

"I have the minny gun," said Keller.

Lortud said, "I was coming to that. Now we're going down that passage to the entrance and try the minny gun on it. If that doesn't work, and from the solidity of the metal, I doubt it, our only chance is to wait till they open the place up, and in the meanwhile use the minny gun on them if they come back. I don't think even they can stand that. Stay together. Wallace, you cover our rear with the light, and give warning if you see one of those damned lobsters approaching. You with the other light, keep your beam ahead of us, and let's go."

The little procession moved off, with a "Quiet, there," from Lortud as two of the hands started to speak in low voices. When they reached the division of the passages the commodore asked, "Think this will give you distance enough to keep out of the explosion, Keller? All right, everybody back in that passage toward the stock pen."

The commander set his weapon on its tripod, adjusted it as the light was thrown on the base of the metal door, lay flat, and pulled the trigger. The whole tunnel seemed filled with the flame of praesodexyl and there was a crash that set all the grazing animals cooing. Keller jumped to his feet and rapidly swung the gun down the other passage, while Wallace shot a beam of light along it.

After a minute Lortud said, "No reaction. I bet it disturbed their slumbers, though, and they'll be a little more careful of how they come in on us next time. All right, let's go see how much damage we did that door. Keller, you better stay here in case."

The base of the door was certainly bulged out a trifle, and as Lortud bent to examine the spot he was aware of a current of air that told there had been a minor penetration, but he shook his head. "Not good enough. We could easily use up all the shells we have for the gun without getting through at this rate, and then we'd be defenseless. Come on."

The talker said, "Sir."

"What is it?"

"I think I'm getting something now, in the low angstrom band." He moved from side to side, then back to where the minny-gun shell had struck again. "I hear it when I'm near this hole. Commodore Lortud here. Come in, *Massachusetts*. . . . They want to know if you're all right, sir."

Lortud barked a grim laugh. "Tell them we're all right for the time being, but I don't know how long we will be. We're locked in here behind this metal door, impenetrable to our weapons. The inhabitants are inimical, nonhumanoid, and very dangerous."

The talker spoke into his instrument, listened, and said, "They want to know whether they shall use atomics on the door, sir."

"No. We can't get far enough back in to escape the explosion without getting down into the living quarters of these animals, and I don't want to chance it. We'd lose men. No, I don't think I want them to use praesodexyl missiles either. The jar of that little one from the minny gun was about all we could take in here. . . . Wait a minute, though—talker!"

"Yes, sir."

"I have it. 'Commodore to Captain Pelham: Station three ships at one thousand meters from entrance this cavern. Have helixes in air for emergency rescue. As soon as door begins opening, ships are to commence intense radar and counterradar emission, pulsating, and on all frequencies, beamed at entrance. Good-by until morning.' "

Without waiting for the talker to finish his transmission, he strode back down the passage to where Keller and the rest of the party were waiting.

"I think I've found an out for us," he said, and described his arrangement. "Now let's leave one man here with a light as an outpost and go back to that stock pen and see if we can get some sleep."

Overhead, the pale glow snapped on abruptly, and the grazers in the larger pen began to stir and give their bubbling notes. Lortud snapped up from the floor. "Sleep any, Rolf?" asked one of the hands. "No, but the boss did," said another, and the man on watch came down the passage, with "They're coming. Four of them."

In a low voice Lortud said, "I want everybody absolutely quiet and down behind this partition. They may not come in here until they're sure their grazers are clear. At least I hope that's how they'll figure it."

The animals began to mill around, then, pushing and nudging, shoved toward the passage, and its walls were suddenly streaked with a light which was not that from overhead.

"The door's open!" whispered Keller.

"Give them a minute or two," Lortud whispered back.

From outside there was a high-pitched whistle that rose unbearably until it disappeared above the level of audible sound, then a series of metallic clankings and sharp bleats from the animals.

"Now!" cried Lortud; with Keller at his side, minny gun at the ready, he vaulted the partition and raced for the exit, followed by the men. Four of the lobster creatures were there, writhing on the metal floor, their antennae twisting, their limbs jerking, while on the ground lay several of the hammer-axes and some boxlike instruments with projecting tubes.

"Don't touch them," said Lortud, and picked his way past into the blessed light of day as one of the helicopter lifts came down. He was the last man aboard. As he looked down from the rising machine the group of grazers below was visible, cooing and running about, as though in panic. Two or three of them had lain down and were jerking feebly.

"Radar's got them too," said Lortud. "Talker, contact those other helixes; tell them to send in landing parties for as many of those animals as they can get. Also contact other ships to do same."

Keller gave an exclamation.

Lortud turned hard eyes toward him. "You don't think I'm going to get out of this place without our beef supply, do you?" he asked.

VIII

☐ "*Southern Cross* is the last one," said Captain Pelham.

"That's good," said Lortud. "This seems to be about the last herd in this valley, and I haven't any special desire to try some other place. We might run into the natural enemies of those lobster beasts, and if they're rough enough to be dangerous to them I don't think I'd care for the acquaintance."

"Door opening down there, sir," said the lieutenant on duty at the periscope plates.

Lortud grabbed the intercom. "Communications? Commodore to Louisiana: Join other ships in producing radar emanations against opening door as cover for *Southern Cross*."

"Something coming out, sir."

"What? Let me see."

In one stride Lortud was beside the plate in time to see a long metallic nose built up of faceted angles slowly emerge from the door in the cliff. For a moment it seemed to hang without any visible means of support; then, trailing a streak of blue fire, it dashed for the low-hanging *Southern Cross* at a speed so fantastic the eye could hardly follow it. The watchers saw the projectile strike; at the same moment there was a blaze of flame at the big ship's return fire struck the mouth of the cave. Another door began to open, but was instantly blasted by the *Impero*. The watchers at the plates saw the *Southern*

Cross's landing party racing for their helix, and a line of explosions blossom along the face of the artificial cliff as the other covering vessels anticipaed trouble.

"Signal to all ships," said Lortud. "As soon as *Southern Cross* has recovered her helicopter lift, go up to fifty miles."

"Shall I open fire?" asked Pelham.

"No. There's enough power down there to keep those bastards busy, and I don't want their fire control confused. There goes the helix."

On the plates they could see the *Southern Cross* swing to recover her machine, the compartment yawning open. Above and to the right of it a hole with jagged edges of torn metal showed where she had been hit.

"That looks like a bad one," said Pelham.

Lortud was already asking Communications to get a connection with the damaged ship on visual, and seconds later her captain's face swam and settled into the plate.

"Are you badly hurt?" said the commodore.

"Yes and no," said the Captain, turned his head a minute to say, "Take her up," and then: "The projectile was non-explosive, but it had so much hardness and velocity that it went right through our armor into the spin-room. We have six dead and four injured. The air cutoffs functioned in the damaged compartments and we're space-worthy all right, but I'm afraid the superspeed drive is pretty much of a wreck, and I don't know whether it can be repaired or not. I've got my engineers looking it over now."

"I'll have the *Gloire* send you over a working party. She has some special equipment and technicians."

Lortud cut the connection and turned to the captain. "Dammit!" he said. "That's about as awkward as it could be. We can't very well leave her behind on a planet like this for a relief ship. I suppose I could distribute her people among the others if that drive can't be repaired. I believe that's allowable in emergency, even if it does involve a mixture of nationalities."

Yurka said, "I don't think that will do, Commodore. All the ships have full complements, and the addition of the *Southern Cross's* people would produce crowding all along the line, even if they were split eleven ways. We're so far out that we have a long trip at superspeed ahead of us, and nothing could be psychologically worse than crowding."

"I suppose you're right. What else can we do, though? There isn't another planet in this system that's really habitable."

Captain Pelham spoke reflectively. "When I was a cadet on the old *Baltimore* we made a training run out to the moons of Jupiter in company with the *St. Louis*. She had a bad premature and burned out her main drive. But old Captain Beynon maneuvered alongside her, welded the two ships together along the exterior stress compartments, and brought both in together. I wonder if we couldn't do something like that."

Lortud said, "That was only on rockets, though, wasn't it?"

"Yes, but the *Gloire* has plenty of power."

"I wasn't thinking of that but of the connections. You know stresses build up cumulatively in an irregular object at superspeed, and I'm afraid the welds would give and leave the *Southern Cross* out there in non-existence."

Pelham pulled his mustache. "That's a factor all right. We might build a false shell around both of them to make the combination a sphere instead of a dumbbell—no, that wouldn't do, either, it would take too long, and I doubt if we have the material. Wait a minute, I think I see the answer. We were going on to Hauraki if we failed to get what we needed here. It's only a short trip from here on superspeed, and the joint ought to hold up that long. It's a Class A planet, open and colonized by scientists, and they'll certainly be able to give us any repairs the *Southern Cross* may need."

Yurka opened his mouth, then seemed to change his mind and didn't say anything.

Lortud said, "I think you've got something there, Captain. So much that I'm going right down to Engineering and calculate out how much the connection would stand while I'm waiting for the report from those two."

He swung out. As the door closed behind him Yurka said, "Always has to do everything himself, doesn't he?"

Pelham said, "It's a family trait, I guess. The Lortuds are never afraid to delegate authority, but I never heard of one of them yet who was willing to delegate a job when he could do it himself. Especially when it's a tough job, like this one."

"Uh-huh. Captain, tell me something about this Hauraki place. Is it part of the commercial system?"

"I don't know offhand, but it's easy enough to find out. Is it important?"

"I rather think it is. If a theory I'm just beginning to play with is correct, it should turn out that Hauraki is not in the commercial system, although it's part of the political and even may have a seat on the Council for this galactic region."

Ten hours later by galactic time, though twilight was already falling over the green landscape of the rapidly spinning 2:92111, far below, working parties from several ships were putting the last touches on the joint that held *Glorie* and *Southern Cross* together in one gigantic double sphere, their torches burning bright as miniature stars. Captain Pelham sipped his coffee and said to Keller:

"Rosy, I'm supposed to notify and consult with you, as exec of this ship, but when we reach Hauraki, I want to get the psychological officer over from the *Louisiana* for a visit."

Keller put his own cup down. "Why? What's the matter with Yurka?"

"If I had some wood here I'd touch it. You know very well that he's pulled up everyone who showed the slightest approach to a breakdown. It's just that he's almost too good, and—just before we hit this place he came to me with a confidential report."

Keller said, "I wasn't informed."

"I know. It was on an officer."

The exec's expression became a frown. "I see—or rather, I don't."

"And this morning, as soon as he heard of Hauraki, he predicted that although it's part of the United Planet's organization it would turn out to be outside the commercial system. He was perfectly right."

"Did he give the basis of his prediction?"

"He said a theory of his required it."

Keller thought for a moment. Then: "Paul, this is pretty tenuous, you know. Just what are you driving at?"

"I wish I knew, Rosy. It's just a kind of suspicion. But Yurka's such a very sharp psychologist that he could handle any one of us about as he pleased, and being in the line he is, he hasn't been conditioned like the rest of us. And the development corporations would do practically anything to hang something on the commodore . . ."

"So you want an independent check on Yurka by another psychologist, who also hasn't been conditioned. Okay. But it will have to be done carefully. Let's see; even if they finish that job of tying the two ships together tonight, we won't be going into superspeed before morning. Let's ask permission for an officers' party with the *Louisiana* crowd. During the festivities I'll make an opportunity to speak to Burke. He was in the class just behind me."

Pelham said, "That seems about as good as anything, I guess." He picked up the intercom.

The landing platform at Hauraki was not a flat surface of concrete, scarred with take-off blasts, like those on Earth, but a long, deep trough of some black material filled with bright spicules. As Lortud led the group out of the exit compartment there was a sound of machinery, a section of the black material swung back on a brightly lighted passage, from which emerged a train of pressure cars driven by a girl. Her hair was loose and stringy and her clothes looked as though they had been thrown at her and stuck where they hit.

Lortud stepped forward and saluted formally. "Commodore Lortud," he said. "Permission to land on your planet, and a request for repairs."

"Laboratory Technician Smit," she replied. "This is an open planet, and you have already received your permission while in the atmosphere. Don't waste words. What is the nature of the repairs desired?"

"One of our ships lost its spin-room as the result of enemy action and is only able to go into superspeed for brief periods while attached to another ship."

"We can supply you with a new spin-room. That much is permitted."

"I think most of my crews would like a shot at a recreation area while the repairs are being made."

"Why? Haven't they been properly conditioned?" Laboratory Technician Smit's face suddenly relaxed into a smile. "But very well. I'll arrange it, though I won't guarantee how much you Earth people will enjoy the forms of recreation we have on Hauraki. We tend to be what you would call—intellectual."

She touched an instrument by her side on the seat, spoke briefly into it in some kind of code, and said, "I have arranged matters. Will you take your place in the car, please, and come to the engineering center? Dr. Bradlet has expressed a desire to meet you. You will not need your communications man; we can handle such details, and I will have a driver pick up the rest and take them to the recreation center."

"I'd like it if Captain Pelham and Commander Yurka could accompany me."

"The invitation was for you alone. Will you get in, please?"

"Go ahead, Commodore," said Pelham as Lortud's black brows contracted. The girl cut out all but the first car with the throw of a lever, reversed neatly, and waited till Lortud got in, not saying anything. As they slid smoothly away into the tunnel the captain said, "Courteous lot, aren't they?"

Yurka said, "It's less like discourtesy than an effort to establish dominance. I wonder——"

The car spun smoothly along, plunged out into bright daylight along a road made of the same material as the cradles which had taken the space ships into an alley of tall trees; speeded up, turned right, and after another short run, halted before a low building with a widespreading roof, surrounded by flower beds. A tall but slightly stoop-shouldered man with white hair was busy at a reading spool on a chair under the overhang.

As he heard the feet on the pavement he glanced up, then stood up, with a look at an instrument on his wrist. "Miss Smit," he said, "you are two minutes and fifteen seconds behind your time of arrival. I presume this is Commodore Lortud." He extended a hand. "Will you sit down and indulge in an alcoholic beverage?"

"Thank you," said Lortud.

"We live very simply here," said the tall man, and stepped to the wall of the building, where he pressed two or three in a series of buttons. "I think you may as well continue that volumetric analysis, Miss Smit."

He sat down again. "I suppose you must be one of the younger Lortuds," he said. "I had a good deal to do with your father at one time, because of our mutual interest in excluding the development corporations—he from the E Centauri mines, and we from Hauraki itself."

There was a whir and click, a door opened and two tall drinks appeared on a little shelf. Dr. Bradlet handed one to Lortud and took the other himself.

"I'm Alstair Lortud," said the commodore.

Dr. Bradlet frowned as he sipped. "Alstair? I don't remember—wasn't your father's name Sigus?"

"No. In fact that was my great-grandfather. Do you remember him?"

"Oh dear," said the Haurakian. "I beg your pardon, I'm sure. We live so withdrawn here that I tend to forget that our scientific development has surpassed that of the older worlds. In some respects, that is, only in some respects. Yes, it was your great-grandfather I knew, about a hundred and fifty years ago by galactic time."

"The hell you say!" said Lortud. "Have you found out how to live that long?"

Dr. Bradlet smiled. "I myself am two hundred thirty-four," he said.

"But why not let the rest of the worlds in on the secret?"

"Because their psychic development is not yet adequate to support it. Or for that matter some of the other things we have developed. That was why we were anxious to keep the corporations out—a question to which we found the answer by refusing to join the commercial system. If it were not for Sigus Lortud's advice and help, however, I fear we might not have succeeded in our policy of withdrawal, so you see we owe a debt of gratitude to your family. Dear, dear, that was a long time ago. I suppose that the issue is completely settled by this time."

Lortud frowned. "Frankly, it isn't. Not at all. In fact I don't know whether I'll have any interest left in the E Centauri mines when I get back. I've been away on this expedition quite a while, and the Anthony group are perfectly capable of euchring me out of my holdings during the interval."

"You don't say! I had no idea that this order of problem was still abroad. Dear, dear, another example of our isolation. What ground are they apt to adopt?"

"Oh, I don't know. One of several. Our Council is very strong on capable management these days, and the Anthony group could ask to take over on the grounds of my long absence, for one thing."

Dr. Bradlet sat up in his chair. "But, my dear man! I can help you there, and I'll be only too glad to do it, in memory of the help Sigus Lortud gave me."

"How do you mean?"

"Of course you're not aware of the McGilvray alterant? No, I thought not; we haven't released it generally as yet. Added to your fuel, it will increase the power of your superspeed drive ninety or a hundredfold. I shall be very happy to authorize a supply for you, and get you home in, literally, less time than it takes to tell it." He touched a stud on the arm of the chair and, like Miss Smit, spoke a few words in code, then smiled at Lortud.

"There. A handling machine is already installing a new spin-room in your damaged ship, and by the time the work is finished the fuel alterant will also be in. Now let us relax a little before having something to eat. Do you care for music, or would you prefer philosophical speculation?"

IX

☐ "I was just up to see Eschelman," said Keller. "He's nearly going bats, with a Heisenberg factor to figure in on his new stuff along with everything else."

"Sit down," said Pelham. "That isn't all, either, you know. It tends to exhaust the air in the ship, as I understand it from Lortud, and a factor has to be introduced for that too. So much speed, so much air left. Still, if it will get us home quickly, I'm all for it."

"So's the commodore. He's all for making the maximum speed and to hell with the expenses."

"Well, you can't exactly blame him. At least I don't. These Haurakians are hospitable enough, but I can't say I care for their ideas of amusement. A couple of hours in front of a machine trying to figure out answers to philosophical questions from the data about an imaginary cosmos is hardly my plan for a good time."

Keller laughed. "Yurka was fascinated, though. You weren't in the same room with him, were you? He drew one of the mathematical machines first, and it stumped him completely. Then the attendant shifted him over to philosophy and he began to perk up. The first thing he tried was giving deliberately wrong answers in order to figure out the psychology of the machine, but the machine was too fast for him, and shifted the questions so he didn't know whether he was getting the answers right or not. He says we needn't ever worry about these Haurakians; they're too interested in purely speculative matters ever to care about using their stuff to dominate other peoples."

"I'm glad of that," said the captain. "They could certainly take us apart if they wanted to." He was silent for a moment. "Yurka's probably right. He's very acute."

Keller said, "Has he said anything further about that matter you mentioned—the confidential report?"

Pelham shook his head. "Not a word. I gathered the impression that he was waiting for something definite to happen."

"So did Burke," said Keller. "And that's rather strange too. Paul, psychological officers just don't wait for someone to blow up one of the rocket ammunition chambers; that's what they're here to prevent."

"Yet you say Burke described him as perfectly normal."

"As far as he could tell on such restricted observation. These fellows always have a hedge of some kind like that when you try to pin them down."

Pelham caressed his mustache. "I wonder. Rosy, I'll tell you this much. From the nature of Yurka's report—from its content, he seemed more worried over a long-range danger as the result of psychological maladjustment than anything that might happen immediately. It could be that since we arrived here on Hauraki he's found out something that changed his mind. He hasn't said another word about it."

"I guess that's all for the present, then," said Keller and picked up his cap. "Going ashore, Captain?"

"I don't think so. I've seen about all the parks I want to see for the present, and this amusement of matching your wits against a machine that's built to beat you doesn't have much appeal. The last time that Miss Okly told me my reactions indicated I needed to develop philosophical calm, and that our habit of using traditional Earth names was a barbarous survival. What the hell did she think they conditioned us as fighting men for?"

Commodore Lortud stood in the con of the *Massachusetts* beside his hammock and said, "I have asked for this all-ship visual hookup for a specific purpose. This new alterant in the superspeed fuel chambers promises to get us to the region of home in ten days' run, but it introduces certain special problems and dangers, and I want to be certain that all you captains understand them."

He glanced along the line of eleven pictured faces, and as there was no reply, went on:

"By the use of this alterant we should emerge from the McGilvray superspeed close to our home solar system, but somewhere outside the orbit of Pluto. The calculations cannot be made sufficiently fine to enable us to come out of superspeed within the system without running the danger of striking some planet or satellite on emerging.

"I have accordingly accepted only enough of the McGilvray alterant to take us to that point. With the linkages that had been set up, we should emerge from McGilvray speed at half-second intervals and in single line formation, as we are now. I have no reason to anticipate any difficulty, but if a gap should appear anywhere in the formation I want the remaining ships to proceed on normal superspeed from the region outside Pluto to the region of the Earth without further orders. Then complete the journey on rockets as usual. Is this order accepted and recorded aboard all ships?"

One by one the ships acknowledged and reported ready. "All right," said Lortud. "Six minutes from now, then. At 0950."

He turned and climbed into his hammock, while the con talker took up the familiar chant, calling off the minutes and seconds remaining before the ship took her plunge into the gray void of nothingness.

". . . three seconds—two seconds—one second——"

Crash!

The last fleeting thought that came to most of those aboard before the blackout was that this was something new in the line of superspeed all right.

Captain Pelham came to to find Lortud and one of the lieutenants at the board, while a husky hand was letting down pressures and folding hammocks. He released his own bindings and stood up, feeling strangely groggy.

"Must be getting old," he remarked. "Didn't used to do that to me. Are we in it?"

Lortud had the intercom. "Navigation? . . . Guess there's nobody conscious in there yet." He spoke over his shoulder to the captain. "Look at the screens."

Pelham took one step and stared. "Why, we aren't in superspeed at all! Those are stars!"

"So they are. And if you'll look at this screen you'll see that the other ships are here, too, though from the angle you can't tell whether they all came through. Communications? . . . Nobody there either. Now take a look at the chronometer, Captain."

Pelham glanced, and his face expressed the fact that he had received the second shock of the occasion. "04ZY," he said. "Why, I've been out for nearly eleven days! No wonder I felt punk."

"So have all of us. We must have dropped through from this McGilvray superspeed simply because the fuel ran out. There was no one to operate the controls manually. I'm glad I didn't have all the tanks loaded with that damned stuff or we'd be going yet."

Around the con men were coming to everywhere now, picking up the hammocks with rapid, practiced hands. The annunciator buzzed and said, "Navigation, Holmgren speaking. Somebody has an automatic on us. Please come in on intercom."

Lortud picked up the instrument. "Navigation, this is Lortud. We appear to have gone through our superspeed period unconscious and I want to be sure of our position. As near as I can make out visually, we're orbiting around the sun in line ahead, and there's a planet inside us in the five o'clock 97 arc. I think it's Pluto, but please identify."

The talker said, "Communications calling, sir. Major Purdy."

Lortud changed the connections. "Purdy, Lortud speaking. Get any other ship you can reach and check whether they've been blacked out all through the superspeed period too. Hello, Yurka."

The commander grinned. "Hello, Commodore. That was like being hit with a hammer."

"Yes, I'm glad we don't have to use that stuff often. Captain, look at this. Are you satisfied with the appearance of that group of stars?"

Pelham stepped to the plate and glanced. "No, I'm not. That has every appearance of a cluster, and it's far too near."

"I thought the same." Lortud frowned.

The talker said, "Sir, Navigation says the planet is not Pluto and it's too small to be Neptune. They're checking."

"Tell them to take a bearing on that cluster too."

Pelham said, "I take it you're worried over the idea that this patent fuel may have blown us into some region of the galaxy we don't know anything about."

"You're damned right I am! With nobody conscious to take us down out of this new superspeed at the right time, hell only knows where we are."

There was a momentary silence in the con, punctuated by a few indrawn breaths. The talker said calmly, "Sir, Communications has the *Dent Ardent*. They report that they have all been out for 10.46 days, and that we are not in the home solar system."

Lortud seized the intercom. "Navigation? Hello, Eschelman. Hondschoote beat you to the punch again. He says we're not in the home solar system. . . . Oh, you did know it, did you? Well, where——" He listened for a moment, then put down the instrument and turned a dazed face toward Pelham. "He's pretty sure that we're at the outer edge of the Hauraki system."

Pelham said, "Then we've spent nearly eleven days of unconsciousness covering a distance that ought not to have taken us more than a few minutes at this super-superspeed."

"Or else we've been involved in some damned phenomenon of space curvature. I ought to have Eschelman's stripes for this."

Pelham said, "I don't think so, Commodore. He was dealing with several factors he hadn't been trained in, and which our computers perhaps couldn't handle. I used to be a pretty good navigator myself, and I couldn't find anything wrong with his figures. Besides, they checked pretty closely with those from the other ships. You'd have to break all the navigators in the squadron."

"I suppose so. Well, what's the next step? The only thing I can see is plot a course for home at normal superspeed, without trying to use this trick fuel." He turned to face the lieutenant who had come in with a salute. "What is it, Hassinger?"

"Sir, you requested to be informed at once if our supplies became low for any operation. After we came out of this superspeed I examined the air tanks. We have only enough for three weeks' run at superspeed."

Pelham whistled softly. "And we're at least eighteen weeks from Earth on normal superspeed," he said.

Lortud looked at Hassinger as though he meant to bite him in two, but when he spoke it was mildly enough. "Check with the other ships and see if they show a similar status on air supply," he said. "I suppose there's no chance of reconversion."

"I've allowed for that, sir. You see, we lose a small

amount every time we operate the subnuclears, and another small amount every time we jettison inconvertible waste."

"Very well." Lortud's voice was almost a snarl as he turned to Pelham. "I hate it like hell, but I guess there's nothing left to do but go back there and ask the Haurakians to bail us out. Talker, call Navigation; tell them when they have checked this as the Hauraki system I want them to set up a course for Hauraki itself, on rockets."

He stood silent for a moment, watching the plates glumly. The intercom buzzed; he said, "Lortud," into it, then, "No, I'll come up there," and swung to Pelham. "There's a message of some sort coming through from that scientific madhouse. I'm going up to Communications."

He strode out. Pelham turned to Yurka. "I don't blame him for being a little—— What are you grinning for?"

"Because this is just what I expected. My theory required it."

Up in Communications, Major Purdy was explaining: "They're using a long-range excitation beam and Universal code. It's too far to pick up on voice. I've already identified ourselves. Here it comes."

He bent over the chattering machine and ripped off the blue sheet. It read:

WHY HAVE YOU RETURNED TO OUR SYSTEM? REQUEST YOU WITHDRAW WAR VESSELS AT ONCE.

"Nice about it, aren't they?" said Lortud. "Tell them: 'Return due to technical error in handling your new fuel. Request permission to land for emergency supply of air.'"

The machine clicked off the message. One of the hands said, "Sir, the *Triumph* is calling, and wants to know if their observation showing us in the Hauraki system is correct."

"Tell them that if it isn't there's something wrong with their instruments. What are we getting now?"

The printer set down:

HAURAKI COUNCIL REJECTS FURTHER CONTACT. YOUR CULTURE LEVEL TOO LOW ON EVIDENCE OF YOUR PERFORMANCE WITH OUR PHILOSOPHICAL MACHINES AND FAILURE TO HANDLE MCGILVRAY FUEL. REQUEST YOU WITHDRAW AT ONCE.

"Why, they can't get away with that!" exclaimed Purdy. "It's contrary to the U.P. convention. We're an official squadron in distress and they're an open planet."

"I'm afraid getting away with it is precisely what they can do," said Lortud. "They're not under the commercial convention, and they've fulfilled their duties under the political by giving us even more than we asked for when we were there. However, let's make one more try. Send them this: 'We have only three weeks' supply of air, insufficient to reach home.'"

Purdy fed the message into the machine, then said, "Couldn't we just run a fast approach into their atmosphere and take in the air we want?"

"There's nothing I'd like better. Those high-hat academicians make me want to use boiling oil, even the mild form you find back on Earth. But it won't do. If they're good enough to have that McGilvray fuel alterant you can take it that they've got enough more to make their ejection order stick."

The machine began again:

THREE WEEKS MORE THAN AMPLE TO TAKE YOU TO CALLA OR URANIA, OPEN PLANETS OF YOUR CULTURE LEVEL. BOTH IN SAME SYSTEM, STAR H.D. 87987. CO-ORDINATES FOR REACHING IT FROM YOUR PRESENT POSITION AS FOLLOWS . . .

"I guess that's that," said Lortud and, as the machine reeled off the calculated course, picked up the intercom. "Navigation? Take a look at the star catalogue, will you, and tell me about Calla and Urania, both of them planets of H.D. 87987. I'll wait."

Purdy said, "I thought the old chap down there on Hauraki was so friendly to you."

"You'd be friendly to a dog, too, but you wouldn't let him sleep on your bed." He held up a hand, then put down the intercom. "Urania's a green-sky planet, and a theosophical religious colony at that. I guess we go to Calla. It's a Californian foundation, but at least that's American."

X

☐ The door of the landing compartment opened, and Lortud, flanked by Pelham, Yurka, and the escort that had been requested as they came down through the atmosphere, stepped out on the landing platform. Two shapely drum-majorettes flung batons aloft into the calm twilight; the band burst into the exciting strains of the "March of the Planets," and two files of gorgeously uniformed soldiers marched forward to rank themselves on either side of the visitors from Earth.

Ahead, in letters of fire that seemed to paint themselves across the sky, appeared the words WELCOME TO MENDOTA: CALLA'S LOVELIEST CITY. Beneath them tall trees waved to the slightest of breezes, still green in the falling light, and there was a shimmer of water visible, illuminated like the trunks of the trees, from some unknown source. Gondolas glided on the water, each with its own subdued light.

"What did you bring the speaker for?" said Pelham, putting his face close to Yurka to make himself heard over the racket of the band.

"Because the commodore came without his talker," said Yurka.

The band finished with the "March of the Planets" and the drums gave a couple of tentative taps. "But he doesn't need communication with the ship for a reception like this," said Pelham.

"No?" said Yurka as the band went off into "The Bird Dance," and Pelham saw his face was grave.

Ahead, the band split apart, a whistle shrilled above the music, and the soldiers faced inward with grounded arms. Through the lane left by the band advanced a woman who seemed to have stars in the long dark hair that fell to her shoulders. Her gown was as low in the front as it could be without falling off and as diaphanous as it could be and still be called a garment, and she had everything it took to be dressed like that. She glided toward Lortud and, with a smile on one of the most beautiful faces any of the Earthmen had ever seen, held out her hand.

"I am Hita Vivar Arossa," she said, "mayoress of Mendota, and I welcome you, Commodore Lortud."

"Glad to be aboard," said the Commodore, and turned to present Pelham and Yurka. Hita Vivar Arossa favored each with a warm pressure of the hand, then took Lortud's arm.

"If you will follow us," she said, "we have prepared a small reception for you."

They were near the edge of the water, which revealed itself as a smooth lake studded with islands. Violins began to play somewhere. The mayoress of Mendota led the party along a path like velvet under the feet, round a clump of trees that looked like a banyan but had flowers at its base, and they saw spread at the water's edge a table, glittering with crystal and silver. There was a place for each of the Earthmen, and at each alternate place a girl, like Hita Vivar Arossa both in being dressed revealingly and in having something to reveal.

The mayoress led the way to the head of the table. "I will have you on my left, Captain Pelham," she said. "This is Zanday Maniu Banita, one of my councilors, who will be your partner. And this, Commander Yurka, is Iren Tenally Momenna, another councilor, who will be yours." She raised her voice and clapped her hands. "Let the others introduce themselves."

Yurka found himself looking into a pair of extremely blue eyes under a mass of blond hair. "Are all your councilors women?" he asked as they took their places.

The mayoress touched a stud at the side of the table and the violins began again, now accompanied by a wind instrument which might have been a saxophone with a singularly sweet tone.

"Oh yes," said Iren Tenally Momenna. "That is, I think there's a man councilor at Hodell, but that's hundreds of miles from here."

Waiters began moving along in back of the tables, filling the tall crystal goblets. The mayoress leaned across. "I was just telling the commodore that after the reception we will go for a sail on the lake," she said. "If you would prefer another partner for the evening, please ask her."

"Thank you," said Yurka, and turned to his own partner again. "I'm interested," he said. "How does it happen that the women hold all the offices?"

Iren looked at him. "Why, we have to pass a beauty examination to be elected, of course. Our geneticists made that part of our constitution. Look at Hita Vivar, there. She's not even a native; came from Earth only about two years ago, and she's already a mayoress, and will probably go on to the District Council. But she's so——"

Yurka suddenly said in a loud flat voice, "Commodore, I don't think I'd drink much of that wine if I were you."

Faces turned toward him, Pelham's astonished one over a goblet he already held.

Lortud's voice was cold. "Why not, Commander?"

"Because this place is a trap; a worse trap than Kushan. I've got the whole picture now, and my theory's airtight."

Hita Vivar was looking at him with big luminous eyes. "No," she said. "I'm not trying to——"

"I know you're not," said Yurka. "You can't help it. You've been conditioned too. I know exactly the program. You're supposed to take him out in one of those gondolas, and then keep him all night, and then stretch it out into more days and nights and weeks. And he's supposed to see that the men are enjoying themselves, too, and not to care too much. He's been conditioned that way. And by the time we all get back to Earth the corporations will have their hooks in the E Centauri mines, good and solid."

Lortud's voice was still cold. "I think you owe me an explanation, Commander—also one to our hostess here. And you had better make it good."

"All right, it will be. When you started out on this expedition, you and every fighting man in the squadron were psychologically conditioned to remove your inbred stops against violence and killing—any kind of *Schadenfreude*—weren't you?"

"Of course, but——"

"Let me finish. Who conducted that conditioning?"

"The Medical Board, as it always does."

Yurka said, "Has it occurred to you that people like the Anthony Corp. could reach someone on the Medical Board?"

"Do you mean that I was wrongly conditioned?" Lortud's frown was that of a man not quite able to grasp what was being said.

"I mean a hell of a lot more than that. I mean that practically every man in the squadron got a dose of this special conditioning, over and above what he needed to make him a good fighting man. Beginning with DeSantis as supply officer, when he didn't give the squadron enough food and water to make the return trip in one hop. Then Hondschoote, who proposed the ingenious plan of stopping off at that damned planet where you nearly got caught by those lobsters instead of going to Hauraki direct. And yourself, Commodore; the use of that special fuel alterant at Hauraki, something you didn't know anything about, was really an irrational act."

The music had stopped. Down toward the end of the table one of the members of the escort was embracing his partner as they drank from each other's goblets, and the pair next to them were laughing as they watched. Lortud said slowly, "You make something of a case, but not a very good one, Yurka. Why couldn't they just have conditioned someone in the fleet to shoot me and get me out of the way?"

"And have him subjected to psychic examination, and their participation brought out afterward? No, they wanted a foolproof scheme. They wanted to involve you in a series of incidents that would take you from planet to planet over a period of time long enough for them to operate at home. I imagine they rather hoped that you would come a cropper somewhere, but they had to predispose you for courage and ingenuity in addition to what of those qualities was latent in your mind already. Even conditioning can't overthrow a latent pattern, you know, only intensify it, or change its direction. So they built into your mind a choice-pattern that would bring you through all right probably, but only after a long time." He laughed. "The only trouble was, they couldn't condition your psychological officer, and they happened to get one who had read the ancient literatures."

Down the table one of the escort and a girl moved toward the water's edge and a gondola, arms around each other. Lortud said, "What do you mean?"

"I mean that they built into your mind a choice-pattern, when decisions had to be made, that was probably suggested by the fact that your remote ancestors were Greek and you were going on an expedition against a place called Ilya. You have been acting out Homer's *Odyssey* in modern terms."

Commodore Lortud passed a hand slowly down his face and seemed to be struggling within himself. "Yes," he said. "I read it once—long ago. We all do in our family."

"The planet catalogues back on earth are much more complete than anything we can carry on a space ship," Yurka went on remorselessly. "They could easily select those that in some way fitted the pattern of the *Odyssey* and introduce into your mind only a slight predisposition to go there. With the latent *Odyssey* pattern at the back of your mind, you'd be sure to choose as they wished. What was the first place Ulysses visited on his return from Troy, or Ilium? The island of Ismarus. That made it certain that when you found a planet named Asmara in the star catalogue you'd go there rather than any other place."

Lortud said, "I see. And while I thought I was choosing these places on technical grounds, I was really following orders? Is that it?"

"Pretty much. They got you to the island of the lotos-eaters and the Cyclops. Of course they couldn't hit it on the button every time, but——"

Lortud made an impatient gesture. "And where are we now, then?"

"The island of Circe," said Yurka. He jabbed a finger at the mayoress. "She was sent out from Earth, conditioned to live the part. The dates check. And I'll bet all the bathing suits in California that this wine has something in it beside just alcohol."

Hita Vivar Arossa had both hands before her face. Now she said softly through them, "No. Oh no. I'm sorry if it's true, I only wanted——"

Lortud stood up. "I have a wife," he said, as though the words were being wrung out of him, "and I'm going home to her—now." He faced Yurka fiercely. "Is that a dictated decision?"

"No," said Yurka. "I think you're out of it—— Grab her!"

The mayoress had suddenly flung herself from her chair and started to run, but she took only two or three steps before Lortud and Pelham had her arms. There was a tinkle of broken glass; the two councilors screamed, and Hita Vivar twisted in the grip of the Earthmen. "Ship, ship," said Yurka into his speaker. "Double landing party. Emergency."

In the background were shouts and the sound of running feet. "They've got the mayoress! Call the police!"

Part of the escort were forming around the leaders, dragging three or four with dazed, uncomprehending faces, who had evidently been drinking the strange wine of Calla.

"Come on!" Lortud's voice rose above the tumult, and at a stumbling run they were making their way along the smooth path to the landing platform. Somewhere behind, where figures moved among the dim lights, a shot was fired and went pinging past, but there was a cry of "Don't shoot, you'll hit her!"

"Let me go, let me go," Hita Vivar cried, and Lortud said, "Shall I?"

"No," panted Yurka. "We've got to take her back to Earth and put her under psychic examination. It's the only way we'll ever prove anything."

Ahead on the platform another landing compartment came down with a clang of metal, and the landing party began to spread out in skirmisher order, weapons ready. A beam of light shot past from the mass of the ship overhead, and they were inside the compartment. Hita Vivar Arossa collapsed, sobbing.

"What will they do to her?" asked Lortud.

"Nothing," said Yurka. "The psychic will show what has been done to her and who did it. Then they'll let her go; she can even go back to Calla if she wants to—but I can think of a few people who might try to persuade her to stay on Earth."

The air lock hissed and swung open. "Shall I lift off?" asked Pelham.

"At once," said Lortud.

A lieutenant met them in the corridor with a salute. "Sir," he said, "the *Bayern* reports trouble in her main generator room. She has been in touch with ground here, and they don't have a shop capable of handling that type of repair here, as this is a non-technical culture. But Commander Eschelman has been looking at the catalogue, and he says that in the system of Beta Herculei they have a planet which could do the job. It's only a short run, and the *Bayern* requests that we stop there."

Lortud looked at Yurka. "You're practically commander of the squadron now. Is this another conditioning job?"

Yurka said, "Probably. What type of star is Beta Herculei? That sounds like an awfully bright one."

The lieutenant said; "It's a B type, but the planet is some distance——"

"That is, a very hot star." Yurka turned to the commodore. "They're getting rough. Do you know what the identification is in the pattern of the *Odyssey?* It's Trinacria, the island of the Sun. And you know what happened to Ulysses there."

Lortud gave a wry grin. "Unfortunately I do. He lost most of his ships and nearly all his crews there. I see what you mean."

He swung toward the lieutenant. "Signal the *Bayern* to land here on Calla and await a relief ship with repair materials. The crew will enjoy themselves. The rest of the fleet will proceed Earthward at once. The Council will probably give me hell for leaving a ship behind, but this is one time that Ulysses is going to get home before the suitors have eaten up everything he owns—and with his crews in one piece."

www.ingramcontent.com/pod-product-compliance
Lightning Source LLC
LaVergne TN
LVHW041622070426
835507LV00008B/403